TEA AT
MISS CRANSTON'S

TEA AT
MISS CRANSTON'S

A CENTURY OF GLASGOW MEMORIES

Collected and compiled by

ANNA BLAIR

BIRLINN

This edition published in 2013 by
Birlinn Limited
West Newington House
10 Newington Road
Edinburgh
EH9 1QS

www.birlinn.co.uk

First published in 1985
by Shepheard-Walwyn Ltd, London

ISBN: 978 1 78027 112 5

British Library Cataloguing-in-Publication Data
A catalogue record for this book is available from the British Library

Typeset by Planman ITES (India) Pvt. Ltd., New Delhi
Printed and bound by Grafica Veneta
www.graficaveneta.com

CONTENTS

ACKNOWLEDGEMENTS

I am grateful, not only to those who shared with me their recollections and agreed to be named in the text, but also to those who preferred to blush unseen under the *nome de mémoire* selected for them.

I dedicate this book to them and also to Patricia who died during the writing and who, at nineteen had not lived long enough to have a great store of memories, but who left glorious ones to herself for her friend to carry into their old age … also to Margaret and John for long friendship and, in the year of her ninety-fifth birthday, to Connie who first called me a writer.

Anna Blair

INTRODUCTION AND
HISTORICAL NOTE

There are some periods which become associated with the name of a feature, a movement or a person dominant during its lifespan – the Churchill Era, the Iron Age, the Thatcher Years, the Enlightenment.

On a more domestic scale, when one speaks of the days of the Glasgow Tearooms, the name of Kate Cranston springs to mind, that lady presiding, as it were, over the civic teacups and cakes. She conjures up a vision of part of the city's lifestyle from the 1890s to the middle years of the twentieth century.

This book is not about Kate Cranston: its pages are simply meant to convey a picture of those years in Glasgow when tearooms were in their heyday, when tramcars clanged and shipyard hooters counded, when some children ran barefoot and others walked the west-end parks with nursemaids, when music-halls were popular and pavements were checkered with peever beds. In short, what it contains are the recollections of elderly Glasgow men and women, of many aspects of their lives: at home, at school and on occasion (just one memory among a host of others) of being taken, as a treat, for Tea at Miss Cranston's.

Nevertheless, since her name is in the title, let's set the scene with a word or two about that doyenne of the city's tea-shops, where she catered for grandmothers in bonnets or cloches, little girls in trubenized collars and, in the early days, for small boys in velvet suits and crocheted collars. An early twentieth-century girl remembers:

> When I went for tea at Miss Cranston's my mother would be wearing a long dress with a nipped-in waist and brush-braid round the hem to stop it getting tattered on the pavement. It was always long dresses. D'you know that when I was a wee thing, of all of my mother I could only ever see her feet ... and her face. Nothing between the two. I only knew she wore knickers because I saw them on the kitchen pulley.

Kate Cranston's lifetime spanned all those changing fashions. She was born in 1849, the daughter of the owners of the Crow Hotel in George Square. Little is recorded of her young life, but by the 1870s, seeing her tea-merchant brother Stuart offering tastes of his different blends to his lady-customers at his Argyle Street premises she was inspired to go a step further and open her own place below Arthur's Hotel at 114, Argyle Street, providing not only the tea but also dainty snacks and cakes, and a pleasant room in which to linger over them. The enterprise prospered and expanded when, as a wedding present in 1892, she was given the whole of the Arthur Hotel building to develop, Argyle Street at the time being the main shopping area of the city with the elegant Daly's store there.

At forty-three Kate married John Cochrane, a Barrhead man of thirty-five who had the wealth to allow them to move in musical and artistic circles, where they met Alexander Reid, who had lodged for a time with Van Gogh and been painted by him. They knew the Walton brothers artists and the young architect-designer Charles Rennie Mackintosh. Kate was also now in a position to indulge her ideas for the fine furbishing of her home and tearooms.

The couple settled first at East Park in Carlibar Road, Barrhead, a roomy semi-detached house which Kate invited George Walton's company to decorate. After a century, the hand of his associate Mackintosh is still to be seen in the elegant and gracious drawing-room, which generations of occupiers have appreciated sufficiently to keep almost exactly as it was originally, with slender white columns, trellis work and stained-glass featuring in the oriel window area, seating still upholstered in Art Nouveau fabric, a fine fireplace and overmantel and handsome plaster-work on ceiling and frieze.

Kate was into her stride now. She opened a chain of tea-rooms, and, having found the style of Rennie Mackintosh in total sympathy with her own discerning taste, commissioned him to design the interiors of other strategically placed establishments like The Willow in Sauchiehall Street and those in Ingram Street, Buchanan Street, Argyle Street and Renfield Street. Glasgow was in its great tearoom period and Cranston's egalitarian doors were open alike to suburban ladies, working-class sweethearts and maids on half-days off, all enjoying their favourite rooms – the White, the Blue, the Dutch etc – in the different restaurants.

By now Kate and John Cochrane had taken on the more imposing mansion of Househill on the bank of the Levern, where they employed indoor and outdoor staff and also, once again, the talents of their protégé Rennie Mackintosh. 'Hoosel', as local people called the place, became a prime example of the designer's unique spatial, slender-lined and light-filled style.

There are still those in Barrhead who carry mind-pictures of Kate, living and entertaining as 'the lady of the Big House', and setting off for Glasgow of a morning with her husband in carriage-and-pair. Somewhere on the journey, it's said, she shed the persona of Mrs Cochrane and became Kate Cranston.

> Quite a wee madam she was s'posed to be at the tearooms... strict but fair' they said she was...went round her places every day and made her staff hold out their hands for her to inspect. People said she had her kitchens white-washed every week. And there was a notice in the Ladies' Room ... 'Would ladies

please refrain from combing out their hair, as there have been complaints of hair being carried away on people's skirts'. Must have been quite an operation to take down long hair, comb it out and put it up again!

Tea at Miss Cranston's in Mackintosh surroundings was the great treat for upwards of half a century in the city. John Cochrane, whose circumstances had allowed this social flowering and artistic patronage to take off, died in 1917. Kate herself lived to be eighty-five and died in 1934, the very year that fire swept through the grand Mackintosh masterpiece at Househill. Her grave is in Neilston Cemetery.

Present generations can be grateful not only that they can eat in the restored versions of The Willow Tearooms, but to Kate Cranston for encouraging the genius of Rennie Mackintosh, allowing it to emerge as part of the distinctive Glasgow Style, an enduring part of European artistic history.

Having sketched something of the life of Miss Cranston, we can now turn our attention to the many other facets of vibrant life, not only in the city, but in the wider world of the days when she was Queen of the Tearooms.

The days of George III and Robert Burns seem astonishingly close when one hears a man of ninety-five speak with a clear memory of a loved grandfather born in 1797. In this book there are a few such memories, but for the most part it contains personal recollections of events and lifestyles from about 1890 onwards. Focussing mainly on the Glasgow of the first half of the twentieth century, recollections are spiced with the older memories of one or two who are, as one 88-year-old put it, 'a kick out of the nineteenth'!

Before the turn of the twentieth century, Glasgow was enjoying an industrial and a social boom in a wide variety of fields.

Its wealthy merchants lived in mansions on the outskirts of the city, its middle classes in spacious stone tenements of several apartments, and its poor, whose mass employment produced the goods for the prosperous, were herded into homes of one or two apartments without bathrooms, and with only a shared outside WC. These warrens gave children either clean, decent and virtuous backgrounds, or little chance of any worthwhile future, depending almost entirely on the smeddum, health and energy, or lack of them, in their mothers.

After the first year of the new century, Queen Victoria was dead and, with her, a social and moral way of life which had been on its way out for fifteen years. The cheerful and indecorous prime of the Prince of Wales had had its heyday during that tailing-off period and Edward was into his declining years even by the time of his own coronation. In Glasgow, although theatres and music-halls were still popular, there were other preoccupations. There was a lively new interest in political matters. The Irish question was burning in a city with large numbers of Irish immigrants, so also were those of women's suffrage and the conditions of the working man and his family. There was also, the new film craze which swept Glasgow, bringing over 100 cinemas to the city. But the second decade of the century belongs, without question, to the 1914–18 war. Before it, crowds gathered outside newspaper offices to hear news of its approach. After it, a generation of girls was left mourning the dead boys they might have married. During the war everything that happened was in aid of it, in spite of it, or because of it.

The armistice brought unbelievable relief and the certainty that the ordinary man, as well as his officer comrade, was now surely worth the dignity of a decent standard of living. But the euphoria was short-lived. The 1920s and 1930s brought disillusion and depression to all except a relatively small number who were able to carve out careers and establish business. While their ladies chatted in Glasgow's tearooms, maids tidied up for them at home. In the years between 1923 and 1938 there was never less than ten per cent of the available workforce of the city unemployed. The day of the Red Clydesiders had arrived.

The picture was not of unrelieved gloom, even in the General Strike of 1926. The traditional humour of Glasgow may have become wry and pungent but it was never totally lost. These were also years of the Charleston and the Black Bottom, the Big Bands and the barely affordable ballroom dancing lessons at the McEwans' studio.

There were social improvements too, wider suffrage, improved housing and better provision for the needy, with the children who had shivered into the 1930s barefoot trudging out of them in decent boots or shoes. Other events marked the 1930s; two to sadden, four to cheer. There were the launching of the *534* as the new *Queen Mary* and the celebrations in 1935 to mark King Geroge V's Silver Jubilee. There was his death a year later and, after the trauma of the abdication of a king well-known and loved in Glasgow, his quiet brother's coronation. As a final fling before the next war, came the defiantly brave Empire Exhibition of 1938.

As the teen years of the century belong to the First World War, so the 1940s belong to the Second World War and its demands on civilians. Employment was full and the clang of hammers was heard again on the Clyde. Life on the home front was brisk and busy. This time people set about their war more soberly, better aware of what fighting men were facing, with air raids overhead and radio war correspondents bringing reality into the living room. Civilians served as air raid wardens, fire-watchers and home guards, and women who had been 'silver-served' a year before in Cranston's or Miss Buick's tearooms now rolled up their own sleeves to serve meals in station canteens and church halls.

Indeed, perhaps the most enduring memory of war-time Glasgow to overseas visitors was the huge reputation the city enjoyed for hospitality.

The end of that war saw the beginning of great changes in Glasgow. In spite of continuing rationing and shortage, long-awaited national reforms brought dramatic improvements to the physical wellbeing of children in a city which had long been a health blackspot. A restructuring of education opened doors to an entirely new stratum of society and threw some of the old social groupings into the melting pot. Massive housing programmes transplanted people from decaying tenements to new homes with modern amenities, although these were often set in soulless wildernesses with none of the old 'heart' in them.

More recently there have been efforts to reinstate community spirit by providing centres, halls and corner shops, in what should have been maturing districts. But the 1960s and 1970s are not really the stuff of this book. The soaring beauty of fine bridges, road patterns and cleaned stone belong to an era that will be remembered by the elderly of the future. Besides, in spite of the great swings of mood and economic circumstance there was, until the mid-1960s, an underlying unity of outlook and a common acceptance of what constituted the 'right and proper' throughout the century. When new freedoms lessened certainties, there came to be as many views of life as there were people to hold them.

Many books have been written about the great men of Glasgow, magnates and merchants. This one tells not of their achievements, but of how their nightshirts were washed, which games their children played in the street, how their labourers lived with eight children in an single room, and how their wives bathed such families with kettles of water in zinc tubs in front of the kitchen fire. Much of it is told in the words of those very washerwomen, labourers, or game-playing children who splashed in the tubs, all of whom have delighted in dredging back to mind the days of starched pinafores, top-hatted schoolmasters, young laughter in tenement closes and even the tender memories of two generations of 'lost boys'.

So, with Kate Cranston lending her name to the teapot and cake-stand period in what was the Second City of Empire, let us turn to the recollections of those whose lives overlapped with hers.

TEA AT MISS CRANSTON'S

I

UPSTAIRS HAD A GASOGENE

It is over 200 years since tenement Glasgow first began to rise to house the influx of country folk abandoning the quiet plod of life in clachan and hamlet, bent on finding their fortunes in the new manufactories on the banks of the Clyde. These houses supplied a want then, and have done ever since, for even today you would be hard put to it to find a Glasgow man or woman over fifty who has never lived 'up a close' in a city tenement. Certainly, of the army of raconteurs for this book, life in so many rooms-and-kitchen was a mystery to very few.

The house where Mr James Shaw was born in 1895 had stood for a quarter of a century before that, and he has made his forays into a long life full of variety and interest from one or other of four tenement homes since then . . . the third generation of his family to occupy such a house.

> My grandpa used to point out to me where he'd lived near Glasgow Green, two stairs up, five houses to the landing, one room to a house. I've aye lived in tenements mysel' but no' a single-end like him.

Mr Jim Lillie, although on the other hand long-since transplanted to the suburbs, remembers his city-centre origins too, and his playing days there.

> I lived as a wee boy up behind Sauchiehall Street, where the Rennie Mackintosh Art School is now . . . played moshie there.

Whatever else has often had to be said about them, and how

3

ever scunnered some of their tenants may at times have been, they were, and are, versatile houses and whether single-end or one, two, three, or more rooms-and-kitchen, they could absorb great spawns of mixed offspring.

> The eight of us in our family lived in a room-and-kitchen till I was fourteen, and never a day passed but my mother talked about the big house we were to get some day . . . maybe a three-apartment!

I. THE KITCHEN OF THE SINGLE END

The basic unit of the tenement was the kitchen, the single-end. This 'solo studio' of the nineteenth century was one apartment, with a four-by-six-foot recessed sleeping area where much of the family store of worldly goods was stuffed under the bed. The rest of the apartment served as kitchen, dining-room, parlour, playroom; and workshop for whatever activities any of the tribe might enjoy.

> There was Mother, Faither, mysel', Willie and the wean in our house before we flitted to the room-and-kitchen. Me an' Willie slep' on the wheelie bed you hurled out from under the big bed at night. The wean (that would be our Annie) was in a wooden crib, there was a kitchen table and just the two chairs an' a bench . . . there was a dresser wi' a bunker, a press in the corner and a pulley.

Whatever of their possessions were not under the bed were arranged on and under the shelf running along above the dresser . . . crockery, ashets, jelly pan, bowls, string-box and tea-caddy.

Then moving round the room, Jack Wilson's memory reached washing and cooking arrangements . . .

> The cold tap . . . just *cold* mind . . . was on the jaw-box (that's the sink). We washed at the jaw-box with water out the kettles at the fire. We'd no range, just an open fire, but wi' hobs. For lightin' we'd gas jets and mantles.

Most rememberers though were brought up with ranges, a luxury in the 1880s but, for perhaps eighty years after that, the heart of home for generations of folk. They were simple at first with a basket-fire and side-ovens heated from the coals.

> Later you got them with a water compartment that you drew your hot water from, by a wee brass tap. And I mind our last one about 1920 had a black iron hob-top that hinged up and down from the wall alongside. That was called a lifter and it had gas burners and a grill on it and a tap-nozzle for the gas-iron.

And back now to Jack Wilson's memories of his single-end home off Cumberland Street.

> There was no bathroom in that place mind . . . and all the families shared the landin' cludgey.

Few houses in the city's working heartland had inside WCs and where there were, they could be primitive and quaint.

> My aunt in Monteith Row had a queer WC. It flushed when you pulled up a lever from the side. Then the handle just sank when you let go. There was no wash-basin in that wee closet and no light.

Whether the WC was out on the landing or squeezed into some small dark cubby in a tiny lobby, that, with the kitchen, was the whole extent of the single-end.

II. THE ROOM-AND-KITCHEN

That kitchen of the single-end, with an extra foot or two and some additional refinements, was common to all tenement homes however many more rooms it boasted. So in the room-and-kitchen . . .

> The kitchen was still the place you really lived in.

The second apartment was the Room, and as well as being a sitting parlour for Sunday visitors it slept the children, whatever the mix or age-range.

> Mother and Faither slept in the kitchen bed. The three of us girls slept in the old brass bed behind the room door and the three boys in the recess bed that was in the big cupboard in that room too.

For its role as parlour, the furnishing about 1910 in most homes was horse-hair upholstery and Spanish mahogany with maybe a good table at the window with a chenille cover to save it from sunlight and hullarackit children.

> I mind yon horse-hair that prickled your bottom, and that you pulled out the wee wiry curls from. My auntie had green velvet on hers but it was rough and sore, no' like a dress . . . oh aye, and we had an aspidistra on a green wally pedestal and veloury curtains hangin' from rings on a pole.

In winter at weekends there was usually a fire lit in the tiled grate with its surround and over-mantel.

> No' carved mahogany like in bigger houses, just maybe painted wood wi' a wee bit design. But we'd a brass fender and fire-irons ben the room. Just for show right enough. It was the black ones from the kitchen that actu'lly got used.

Chairs, settee, table, cake stand, cupboard bed, with what one lady calls their 'chiffoneer'; and maybe in a high-falutin' parlour, even a piano and stool . . . all of them sat on, or around, a square of carpet over dark-stained floorboards. And that was the Room.

III. THE TWO-ROOMS-AND-KITCHEN

Upmarket a little, but perhaps in the same street and at an annual rent of £26 10s. in the late 1920s, came the seemly two-rooms-and-kitchen houses. They had virtually three apartments and room for gracious living . . . most children of such homes, where the parlour was the holy of holies, remember it best as the scene of their mother's tightly regulated 'At Homes' for her friends.

> Talk about the Japanese tea ceremony, I doubt there was any more ritual about that than about afternoon tea parties at our house around 1910. Everything was re-dusted (for never a day passed but it was dusted anyway), the fire and the gasolier-jets got lit and a white lace-edged cloth got thrown over the chenille on the big table. And d'you mind épèrgnes? We'd a ruby glass one that was

one of my mother's precious treasures. It went on the table wi' a sprig or two artificial flowers in it.

And there was the best china, the silver tea-pot, cream jug, bowl of sugar lumps and tongs, and perhaps even a spirit-kettle keeping water hot on that 'chiffoneer'. Where the visited and the visiting had aspirations to real refinement there would be a small tray in the lobby for the leaving of the visiting cards.

What I thought was real funny was the way the ladies kep' on their hats when they were at their wee bits of shortbread, or their cherry cake out the cake basket.

So such a house made it possible to entertain with a little style, with the children perhaps brought in to play a piece on the piano and, forbye the chamber-music and afternoon teas, maybe with a glass of limeade from the gasogene.

D'you mind gasogenes? Upstairs had one when I was wee and I thought they must be quite rich. It was a syphon kind of thing in a wire-mesh casing and their papa made soda water in it on Sundays (though mind he was a kirk elder). Then he put in Rose's Lime or lemon juice. That was it ready and he used to say, if you were there, 'Come on and get a drink of gasogene, Hen.'

The main delight of the two-rooms-and-kitchen was having the bedroom . . . the *separate* bedroom, with its privacy and its wee gas fire with the fire-clay pretzels, its starched bed-pawns and its substantial furniture. A woman (no, a lady now) could fair fancy herself furnishing a bedroom.

In our mamma's bedroom there was a wash-stand with the ewer and basin, soap stands, tooth mugs and all . . . everything matchin' in all flowery china . . . even the chantie in the cupboard below. She used to do a funny wee thing, Mamma, she used to save any feathers that came out the pillows when she was whacking them into place with her walking stick, and she saved the feathers in the toothbrush-rack till she'd a wee bundle to put back into the pillow ticking . . . very thrifty Mamma was.

That wash-stand was marble with the back-splash inlaid with coloured bird tiles. There were towel-rails at the ends and a small drawer where Mamma kept a little store of 'braw' soap hardening, to make it last when it was in use.

> We had a bathroom an' all mind, but when my granny or someone came to stay, they didnae have to join in the stramash for washing in the bathroom. But what I mind best about that big flowery basin was the fruit steepin' in it come July, when the jam got made.

Dorothy Laurie was born in 1899 and from the days around 1906 remembers the honey-coloured walnut of her mother's bedroom furniture, the wardrobe heavily carved and big enough to hide in, the free-standing brass bedstead.

And Mrs Helen Stewart recalls the trim of their brass and lacquer bed . . .

> wi' white frilly material and pawns of hand-crochet tied to wee balls along the bed-rail.

Another down-to-earth lady debunks a favourite myth of later years.

> Oh aye, bed pawns. I mind them. You hear folk say nowadays that people in olden times covered up the legs of their furniture for modesty. I never heard such blethers. Half of Glasgow had to strip and dress and maybe bath, boys and girls in the one room. The furniture leg-covers wasnae modesty at all. It was just they liked the frills, and forbye crochet was all the rage. My ma would've put wee dabbie-douces of crochet on anything!

IV. MORE ROOMS-AND-KITCHEN

When a family reached the dizzy heights of tenancy with more than one bedroom, and roamed about in four or more apartments, anything was possible in those airy and spacious houses with their fine plaster cornices and good woodwork. There social life could really ripen. Miss Nancy Reid enjoyed her childhood in a roomy city-centre home in Chisholm Street.

> We'd a great big hall in our house, big enough for two sets of eightsome reels. What lovely parties we had in that place. I lived there until I was married.

Such lobbies are still unbelievably big, certainly to those who live now in 'little boxes made of ticky-tacky'. One young mother recently measured her tenement flat hallway for floor covering and took her gizinties to a carpet store. The salesman shook his head.

> Away home Hen, you've mishured wrong, that's twice the size of my lounge!

By the time you were into this rent-bracket, zinc baths in the kitchen had been left far behind. The name 'bathroom' seems to have had status enough, for in the early days they were scarcely the havens of steam, hot towels and perfume of even thirty years later. Mrs May Milree was fascinated by one she knew as a child in the 1890s.

> I had four maiden aunts who lived near Abbotsford Place. The whole house was pretty old-fashioned and gloomy (though Abbotsford Place was a good address then). But it's the bathroom I mind . . . oh my, that bathroom! It was just a black dark cell place with no light, no gas, no nothing to brighten it except by a wee grille-thing from the close-wall outside. No wash-basin, just a WC and a queer old bath, half built into the wall . . . just a cold tap and a plug. You'd to carry the water in jugs from the kitchen and you'd to take a candle in with you!

And toast yourself off its flame, after the bath, perhaps.

So from one apartment to seven or eight and lobby, that has been the stone, mortar and remembered furbishing of tenement Glasgow for the greater part of 100 years.

V. THE OUTDWELLERS

Not all good folk who brushed out closes, lit wash-house fires and ran down to back greens with baikies of ashes spent their entire lives in tenement communities. Some came in to them from other kinds of house, and some went out from them, when the new suburban semis began to barnacle the countryside round Glasgow between the wars, and from the later 1950s. Maggie Anderson was one who lived her young life in one of the city's outskirt villages.

It was right country in Uddingston then. We had a grand garden wi' chrysanthemums and wi' roses growin' up the wall. And we'd a kind of ramblin' fruit orchard for gooseberries and blackcurrants, plums . . . aye and strawberries . . . and there was an apple-tree by the kitchen door. My mother made a lot of preserves and jam.

I left all that when I got wed to Davie and came to live in a tenement. My, some change! But it was my own wee place and I loved it . . . and I knew I was well off by some, at having an outside toilet that was ours alone.

And from six miles to the south side of the river another bride left a country girlhood:

My wife's family lived in a white but 'n' ben cottage at the Mearns. There was other low whitewashed houses there and milk floats came in from the farms to the Mearns Cross. Now it's a big-big shopping centre and a garage out there.

These came new to tenement life and liked it well enough, but others, to whom it was old, left with little regret.

When we had our room-and-kitchen it was aye a pipe-dream that we were to get a big house some day . . . maybe a *two*-rooms-and-kitchen. Pie in the sky! When it actually happened we couldnae credit it!

When the day of the move came, young Nellie Edgar, fourteen at the time, went off to her work at the weaving-mill from the old house in Wodrow Street . . .

My mother didnae let any of us see the new Corporation house at the Wellmeadow until the day of the flitting. It was her big thing, so's that when we came home that night from the mill or the school, it was to the new place . . . seeing it for the first time. Well see! I walked in that door and there on the floor were beautiful Congoleum squares . . . pink in the girls' room . . . the *girls'* room! And kind of blue for the boys' room. Printed waxcloth it would be without a border, just a square laid in the middle, the way you'd a carpet later on.

And of all wonderful things, a *wooden* bed, after years in an old brass thing!

(Ah Nellie! The world would beat a path now to Wodrow Street for that scorned 'brass thing'.)

... and forbye the wooden bed there was a dressing-table and a wardrobe wi' a mirror and a lovely new bedspread. My parents' room was the parlour too, so they had their bed in it and a three-piece suite. Forbye that we'd a real living-room, separate from the kitchen, and a bathroom. No more tin tubs. And there was the garden.

So some moved in and some moved out. But some remained faithful and, when they flitted, just moved from close to close round their own hub. James McClelland was one of the aptly cried 'flitters'.

I lived in seven houses, all in Bridgeton, between 1918 and 1939. We were aye on the move, sometimes to better houses, sometimes not so good, depending on how we were doing at the time. Mother loved flittin' and she had it down to a fine art. We were in Silvergrove Street, two houses in Muslin Street and four in Greenhead Street. I doubt she would've stopped at that but the war came and she couldnae very well change after that. I mind the landlady arranging about that last house.

'I'll put in hot water and maybe make a bathroom in the attic, and put in the electric an' all, if you'll take it,' says she. It was £26 10s. the year, the rent there, in 1938.

By two years later there wasn't a To Let board to be seen for an unfurnished house in Glasgow, nor has there been since.

Of all the rememberers born before 1940, only two sisters are still part of that tenement world. The rest are surrounded by gardens or landscaped estates.

But the tenements are not empty, for their children and grandchildren have flocked back to redd them up and make their own first homes there ... all part of the tide of Glasgow folk that ebbs and flows to and from the tenements that have always been the city's heart.

2

DAISIES ROUND MY HAT

The photographer of the 1880s swoops under his dark velvet cloth and snaps his fingers at the family group. Breaths are held and, as the cliché says, a moment in time is captured for ever, and with it an array of that era's fashion from infants' to grandparents'. Repeat the process every decade and you have a century of change from bonnet to princess of Wales' feather, button boot to pink sneaker. Well . . . you'd have the gamut right enough, as far as the bien-provided were concerned, but for much of that hundred years there was a broad swathe of Glasgow folk a world away from wool and velvet and starched pinafores.

> I was reared up in Eglinton Street in the 1920s and it was hardgoin' to get claddin' for the five of us weans. Ma went round the toff houses wi' her bundle and if you were lucky she maybe got a pair of boots your size. Other than that, it was barefoot until you got a pair off the parish.

And another glimpse of garb that was a far cry from fancy pin-tucks or feather boas . . .

> I mind my mother goin' her shoppin' wi' the wean in her shawl (there was aye a wean) and I mind the way she swep' the end of the shawl round the baby and tucked it in . . . She never wore a man's bunnet the way some did, all the same.

So for sure, you didn't run barefoot in Eglinton Street or carry your wean in a shawl and then find yourself in a photographic studio all doodied up for a family group. And for the eighty-year span of our direct recollections here, there are brought to mind not only the changes in family fashion, where clothes were bought new or made-up from materials fresh-scissored from the bolt, but also the make-dos and hand-me-downs that came home in the old-clo'es wife's bundle. To march them all past for inspection would take a volume in itself and so a chapter can do no more than flicker through the memories and frame some of the most vivid. In this one it will be enough to glance at children's clothing.

The very earliest picture then is second-hand, and certainly not one captured by the camera. It comes through the diary of Mr Walter Freer and by word of mouth from him to his grandson.

> When I was a lad going to work at eleven year old in the 1860s I had one patched suit and one shirt to wash out at night for the next day, and I had to mend my own boots with scraps of leather found at a cobbler's workshop.

The earliest first-hand memories are those of Maggie Anderson's childhood days around 1892.

> I went to school in Uddingston and I mind my button-hookin' boots and a wee dress down to my ankles. You wore a white pinafore wi' frills . . . a peenie you ken . . . you'd always a peenie. And I had a cloth tammy wi' a button-up coat. Then of course you were right dressed up on the Sunday. 'Every day braw, Sunday a-daw' my mother used to say.

Mrs May Milree has wistful memories of her pinnies too.

> I used to watch my friend Mary Aitken playin' peever in her lovely pinafores and wonder how it was that hers were all crisp and stiff compared to mine. Then I found out her father had a laundry.

But the lady who had been little May, of the limp and second-rate pinnies, did not say whether the beauty of Mary Aitken's pinafores came from constant laundering or maybe from getting the choice of the best that came in for treatment.

The button boots of Maggie Anderson's schooldays were not confined to the pavements of Uddingston and her namesake

Mrs Cathie Anderson has a recollection of hers that still draws an 'ouch' in the telling.

> I've still got my button-hook I had when I was a girl, and I can feel yon wee tweaky feeling yet, when you nipped your leg getting hold of the button.

But, better than the outer garments, others remember the simmits and chemises that went under the wincey-frocks and peenies. And the next-to-skin garb most universally loathed was undoubtedly combinations. Miss Nancy Wall speaks for generations of the tormented, buttoned into combies,

> I hated them . . . all tight and sore between your legs.

And hated they were, for forty years before and after that. But they were only the first of the several layers deemed essential to hap the kidneys and loins.

> We wore drawers . . . just the two legs joined with no middle bit and tied at the waist . . . then top of that umpteen pettis . . . a red flannel one first, with maybe a wee tate black embroidery to it. Then a plain one like enough, and a red-and-white striped one over that. Then we'd bodices with bones in them to support our wee bosoms. Mother thought we'd go to seed without these corset things.

Cathie McMillan confirms that fellow-sufferer's testimony, and still shudders at an imposition she and her sisters had to bear.

> Mother made us knitted petticoats that we called the nightmares. She was great on keeping us warm and she didn't care tuppence that we looked all bumfly in them.

A unisex outfit of the early century and before, was the sailor suit in varying degrees of chic. Around 1905 or 1906 most girls had those or kilted fisher-wife costumes, but the boys were thirled to the fashion for over twenty years. Two school-class photographs, fourteen years apart, show eight of sixteen boys in one, and twelve of seventeen boys in the other, wearing sailor suits in one

form or another, and the unworthy thought occurs that the
boys were arranged for the photo by Miss Whatever, so that
the lower halves of the suits in cheap and wrinkled cotton 'stuff'
were hidden by the shoulders of well-put-on wee lads in decent
sturdy wool with polished boots and braw-knit stockings. There
were accessories too.

> I had a whistle on a cord wi' my first sailor suit, and once, when
> I was a wee soul, I blew it out loud in the kirk. I got a skelpit
> leatherin' for that and they took the pea out my birll!

Older boys at posh schools in the city favoured the sailing
theme too in the summer months, and wore high-buttoning
blazers and panama boaters with school hat-bands. But three
miles from such academies, in the old 'country' borough of
Pollokshaws, the rugged little Willie Stevenson might have
spurned the sailor suit or boater-and-blazer outfits as 'cissy'.

> When I went to the school in 1902 I mind of wearin' wide trou-
> sers down over my knees, and stockin's . . . and you'd yer jaicket.
> No school cap nor nothing . . . just a big bunnet wi' a button.

Sundays went on being 'a-daw' well into the middle of this century and never-a-one of the rememberers but drew a sigh at the
recollection of Sunday bests.

> We always had on Sabbath clothes and when I was fourteen I got a
> nice fur set to go with my mixed-tweed coat . . . a fur pull-through
> tie, a muff and a little fur hat with red cherries. I boasted to all my
> friends in the Bible class that I had all this new for the next Sabbath,
> and when I came down that Sunday morning in my squirrels Pa was
> sitting at one side of the fire and Ma the other. I bounced in, 'My,
> aren't the girls all just going to be jealous of me!'
>   Pa looked at me. 'If that's the way of it just you get back up the
> stairs and change into what you wore last week and see if the girls
> are jealous of that.'

And the black-burning shame of turning up at the church hall
without the new braws is as sore after eighty years as it was that
Sunday morning.

They certainly had their specials for Sunday, and Cathie McMillan's 'specials' were hats.

> Mother was a wee bit hatty and she got the milliner in Clarkston Road to line our straw hats with pink silk, and put daisies round them. We all sat in a row in the church. Ten of us in the pew, the girls all with our nice hats . . . me and Isa and Anne and Minnie. They would all be lovely, but it's my own I mind the best. Isa was pretty. She had wee round rosy cheeks and I used to think it would be lovely to look like Isa. We'd Sunday coats too, but I loved those hats.

All through Edwardian days and beyond, older boys wore Norfolk jackets and knickerbockers, and untidy teenage slouching was discouraged by stiff collars. The 'big-big wide collars, near out to your shoulders' were common to most quarters in the city, but the west-end lads wore them also over the cut-away silver-buttoned jackets they had with their kilts. And, even without either Eton collar or kilt, Willie, the lad of the 'big bunnet wi' the button' has to admit,

> Oh aye, we were a'dressed up for the Sabbath . . . smart turned-out to go to McAlpine's kirk.

But whether from villa or single-end the boys all had one style in common.

> Wir hair was cut to the knuckle.

It was often cropped by fathers, along a line made by the rim of a bowl held with the back of the head firmly into it, although boys from families with money to burn went to have theirs done professionally.

> I remember when I got my hair cut for a penny. I used to get a balloon from the barber in Nithsdale Road.

The boys' clothes, buffed of their Sunday newness, did further service at school, until wrists dangled out of sleeves and suits were passed down the tribal line. But few girls recall turning out on weekdays in the faded glory of Sunday bests.

They were too fancy for school wi' their cape-shoulders and velvet collars. They just got passed on to your wee sister for the kirk and then when there was no more wee sisters they went to the old-clo'es wife.

May Gilmour agrees,

No, no, never your Sunday things through the week. I remember summer Sundays the best. There was a terrible lot of gingham dresses and straw hats with flowers when I was young.

There were infant fashions too before the First World War, and those babies who boasted nannies in dark dresses, stiff collars and cuffs, sat in high wicker prams like tiny rosebuds, in frothing crumples of lace trimming bonnet, pillow and pram covers. And while the rose-bud baby's next-up brother, aged about three or four, was photographed gazing into a goldfish bowl, long hair curling about his neck and shoulders and wearing a white cotton dress with lace inserts, white socks and boots, his small contemporary on inner-city streets was toddling barefoot alongside his shawlie mother.

Throughout these years of Eton collars and flower-decked hats the cotton pinny had had a long innings but by the early teen years of the century it was changing. It wasn't quite out yet though.

I mind of wearing a nice white peenie wi' a square flap. My mother was awful fond of the crochet and my peenies had nice wee crochet bibs on them.

But it was becoming more of a main garment, first as a pinafore dress and then later as the most enduring garment of the century. The full flowering of the slip-over they wore with jersey or blouse, came when the day of the gym tunic dawned. Among the rememberers, the first to mention that ubiquitous and perhaps eternal garment was one who, as young Cathie McMillan, tholed a home-made green one in 1912 when all her classmates were in navy blue.

My mother made it, so I just kept quiet and suffered it.

May Reid had a tunic at the big school in 1916, and the Edgar girls had them around 1919. Nellie Edgar had a vision of their top to toe silhouettes in not only the gym slips themselves.

> We had hand-knit stockings with our gyms. Mother knitted them for the three of us girls. She'd her own pattern eight rows plain . . . one row purl. That made an inch y'see. She just did so many patterns for Nellie, so many for Maggie, so many for Bessie. Didnae need to stop talking to look . . . just felt the ridges.

The century climbed on into the 1920s, 1940s, 1960s and 1970s and on marched the gym tunic with it. Surely not a schoolgirl from 1910 to the present day has survived girlhood without one. Let a 1970s school-leaver have the last word on gyms.

> The one I got when I was in Primary I, did me all my schooldays to Secondary IV. It must've been down to my knees when I was five and well up my bahoochie and straining at the shoulder buttons when I was fifteen.

An investment was that gym.

Other fashions came and went for your average bien wee citizen during those post-war years.

> Boys in my class were into wee navy jerseys . . . 'genzies' we called them . . . all rough and jaggy wi' collars and no ties, sometimes a wee loop and butt'n. You wore them over wide home-made breeks that the wind go'ed skimmin' up come the winter. The toffs in the class didnae wear genzies mind.

There was no whinge in the tone of that 'home-made'. But not everyone was quite so jokoh about having their seams run up on the Singer by a less-than-skeely mother.

> Mother made my clothes till I was well up . . . Did I like that? No indeed I did not. I used to wonder to myself, 'May, are you *never* to get any-thing *bought?*'

It wasn't only their clothes that delighted and tormented the embryo ladies of pre-1914–18 days. Their hair gave them hours of urgent consideration and care and, where the boys were uniformly short-backed-and-sided, the girls were pig-tailed and ringletted, or even almost clothed in flowing cascades of hair that reached their bottoms. All of them . . . Muriel Wotherspoon was sure, except herself.

> I had thin hair, just in wee straggly skinny pigtails, with ribbons on the ends that kept getting lost. The girl in the pew in front of me at the church made me angry at the way she could toss her thick pleats over her shoulders, and when they came flying back, I used to clamp the ends into my hymn book. Anyway, once that girl let out a yell when she stood up for the hymn and I just didn't know where to put myself . . . my mother knew where to put me though.

And the hats that topped or framed the glory of rag-curls or bunches are well-remembered too . . . not so much the woolly pull-ons for school but the Sunday best as recalled in the Edgar family.

> We had our good Sunday hats, the three of us girls. Just shapes they were, really, that did us for years. Say about June, Mother used to take off the velvet band that was for the winter and do them round and round wi' flat silky kind of straw, in and out the brim. Then wi' wee bunches of red cherries or purple grapes and a bit ribbon, that was your braw summer hat for the Secession kirk on a Sunday.

By the 1920s and 1930s a kind of blight descends on children's clothes. They may have been more sensible, easier to live in and launder, but they were certainly less memorable, although there are some visions. Babies' clothes were less frilled and goffered by then . . . infants were, rather, cosy bundles of chilprufe and wool.

> I mind when our twins, Gracie and Em, were wee, my granda' used to call them Tweedle-dum and Tweedle-dee. Just like clootie dumplings they were, in their woolly coats and pantaloons.

Older children too had cast most of the suffocating layers and flounces of twenty years before, and remember simpler garb.

> Skirts were that short that my granny used to tut-tut at seeing wir knees. She'd've been right past hersel' if she'd seen us wi' wir

frocks tucked into wir knickers turning wir wilkies in the school sheds.

Underneath that short skirt or gym, girls in the 1930s were still struggling to peel off the last vestiges of what thirty-odd years before, had been the wee McMillan nightmares.

You had them liberty-bodices, all cotton and fleece and wi' buttons at the hems to hold buttonin'-on suspenders for your long wrinkly stockings . . . though what was 'liberty' about yon I cannae think.

Although the good coats, the liberty bodices and even the scratchy genzies eventually found their darned and well-worn way to needier homes, there were still children who not only never had anything new themselves, but who fell through even the net provided by decent hand-me-downs. Their plight was met by the Parish.

When I was teaching around 1933 it was the time of the slump, and Glasgow was really hit. Lots of the weans were very scantily-clad and off the school many a day, while the clothes they had were being washed or maybe pawned. A lot got free clothing but they stood out like sore thumbs. I just don't know where the Corporation got the shoddy trash they gave these bairns for clothing . . . I just don't. For a time they would be in green issue and later a kind of gingery yellow. Awful. Rough and cheap . . . The teacher got a flimsy saying 'So-and-so's got one pair knickers, one dress, one pair boots' and you were s'posed to keep an eye open to see them being worn. If not . . . 'Where's that *beautiful* dress you got from the school-board?' I had to ask.

Sometimes it wasnae at the pawn . . . 'My ma biled it and now it'll no' go on me.'

But there was a change brewing; imagination and good sense were brought to bear and within ten years you couldn't tell a Corporation-dressed child from any other.

Simplicity, practicality and the need for plenty of garments for frequent changing are the modern principles for children's clothing. Very sensible. But clothes are not cherished as they were, nor are the memories of them. Certainly not as they were in the Edgars' home in the 1920s when economics dictated attitudes. And perhaps the most vivid picture of all, of the way decent Glasgow parents turned their children out, on wages like eighteen shillings a week, is this memory of young Nellie Edgar's.

> We didnae have a wardrobe. In the first place the house was too wee, and then wardrobes were dear things. But there was a big kist in the corner of the lobby and it had wee flap-lid compartments at the sides, for Faither's bowler and the rest of us' hats. On a Sunday night, after wearing our braw clo'es, the lid got lifted and Faither's suit went down first, then Mother's clo'es, then Willie's and Jim's, then Maggie's, Nellie's, Bessie's, then George's . . . and all the Bibles. In went the moth balls and the lot lay there till the next Sunday morning when we all lined up in our undies to get out our braws for the kirk. The boys and girls all got dressed together in the one room and nob'dy thought a thing about it.
>
> After the Sunday school our good shoes got taken from us, all brushed, and polished wi' velvet, then they were put up on a shelf above the lobby door. We'd no slippers, so for the rest of the Sunday evening you wore your school shoes.

Mind that next time you're rummaging in your whole wall of built-in wardrobes for something to wear!

3

NO HOOVERS NOR NOTHING

> Our maids dusted and polished, cleaned brasses and silver, did mountains of dishwashing, black-leaded grates, answered the door, sat in with the children, attended the family at table when my ma tinkled her wee handbell and generally kept the home-fires burning . . .

and they were paid wages varying from eight shillings a month at first mention in 1895, to twenty-five shillings in the early 1930s, and a breath-catching three-pound fortune in 1939. And forbye that, they were to be grateful for their keep.

Some maids were large cogs in the wheels of household management, some small, but whatever part they played their job was either to keep mansion or villa running smoothly in Pollokshields or Milngavie, or to maintain the good ordering of three-storey-and-basement town houses in the likes of Clairmont Terrace. They were paid to bring an atmosphere of calm-sough to the homes of the busy merchant and professional men who kept the city humming. The daughter of one such house remembers.

> Our maids used to come from Islay or other places up north. We usually had a cook, a table and parlour-maid, and a woman to do the rough work . . .

and one of the cogs has *her* say of a maid's life in 1928:

> I was put out to service wi' the Honourable Charles Smithson, and I worked as a kitchen-maid wi' them in the town and then at their country place down Dumfries way. I got twenty-two pound a year for that, an' it was drudgery. I got to see Dumfries just the once, all the time I was there.

Other maids were just wee lassies-of-all-work in two-rooms-and-kitchen tenement houses where there were delusions of grandeur. They changed their garb between morning and afternoon to match the different jobs done by various 'grades' of girl in more pretentious establishments.

> It was a two-rooms-and-kitchen tenement we lived in — you didnae call them flats then. There were my parents and us three children. I think my mother had big ideas because we had a maid even in that wee house. She wore a blue wrapper-thing, white cap and apron in the morning and maybe a thibbet pinny for the dirty work. Then she was all done-up in the afternoons in her black and whites . . . very trim, wi' long streamers dangling from her cap and pinny. That was for opening the door and serving up the tea. She took the baby out too, but here, the joke was that she'd him in a shawl instead of a pram and that took the tone down a peg or two. So she was a poor folks' nanny as well's everything else. She slept in the kitchen bed recess.

The maids themselves needed no lessons in sorting out the caste of their mistresses.

> Aye, there were the toffs in the fancy houses and the wee folk wi' big notions of theirsel's in tenements.

But between the two extremes were the modest households in the spreading suburbs. Says Lily Timlin . . .

> By my time in the 1930s, it was mostly just ordinary nice houses wi' gardens and wi' nice-enough women to work to. You just helped wi' everything, cleanin' and makin' beds and maybe switching the carpets wi' damp tea-leaves. No hoovers nor nothin' then.

These were the middle years of remembered service, but it's not so long since one old survivor of Victorian times used to tell his daughter of his sister's working days as a housemaid.

> He used to talk about her being in service in the 1880s. Once she went on holiday with the family to work in the house they took. It was hard work and after it, her mistress gave her a whole shilling and the weekend off. What a treat!

'It was Hallowe'en,' he used to say, 'and I'll never forget the excitement of her coming home and bringing sweets and an apple for every last one of us. It was luxury I can tell you.'

And another glimpse of life from under-stairs.

It was a big house and I was the kitchen-maid. The house-maids did the rest of the house, and the parlour-maid attended to the family. I helped the cook, swep' the kitchen, washed the black pots wi' scourers, and the copper ones wi' vinegar and salt. I done the dishes wi' washin' sody. Oh and my hands got that raw! I was just a skivvy. Come to think on it, I'm seventy now and I'm still a skivvy. I've aye been that.

and she laughs without malice or resentment.

The thing I got to do that I liked best was sittin' at the big fire making toast for us in the kitchen. Another time I mind of at that place, was me havin' a nice pair of patent shoes that I saved for, and that were kind of precious to me, and I had them on once when the honourable madam sent for me. And did I get lalldy for not having on my right strap-and-button shoes to come into that parlour? I was made to go away and change out them into yon other things.

But there was often an affectionate and long-lasting relationship forged between family and help, that had nothing to do with being set apart, 'them and us'.

Other people had cooks and kitchen maids. We had Nana. Nana came to us about 1899 when she was fifteen to wheel out my brother James in his pram.

And Nana flits into the speaker's memory at every stage of her life.

I remember Nana standing ironing all that broderie anglaise with flat irons, and all those frills with the goffering iron.

Nana used to come with us on holiday to Maidens, just to help with the family.

There were five of us children, always one being wheeled in the pram. Nana seemed to push that pram for years and years.

My mother and father died within a short time of each other when we were still young girls and Nana just came with us when we moved into a flat.

Nana had come to the Wotherspoons in 1899 and, still part of the family, died in the 1970s, at the home of one of the boys she had come to wheel out in the big wicker pram around Maxwell Park so long ago.

Couples who found romance in service at large establishments and had spent years jointly absorbing gentry customs, often brought a distinctive style to their own home lives. Miss Marie Condie looks back,

> I had this aunt and uncle, she'd been the cook in a big house and she'd married the butler . . . my uncle Bill, that was. At Christmas time around 1906 and 1907 all the family used to go to their place in Uddingston and I mind the spit over their fire turnin' slowly wi' a bit roast or a fowl on it. It was great! Then the gas-lights would go down to a wee peep, the door used to open and uncle Bill wo' walk in wi' a big flamin' pudding and the wee sprig of holly on the top.

But the niceties of life in douce homes, with worthy Glasgow matrons training up maids to be quiet-spoken and lady-like, sometimes had less seemly secrets. And about 1910 a group of alert citizens began to be aware of one of the hazards of being a young woman in service in Glasgow . . . a young woman who, however cherished a daughter on a Highland croft or in a mining village somewhere, could be anonymous and unprotected in the city. They heard clash of things that went on secretly under the attic roofs of west end houses.

> You aye got wee, wee attic rooms. But if you came off a big family, sharing your kitchen bed wi' maybe three sisters, you thought you were in heaven up there wi' a room and a bed to yoursel', three or four empty drawers and hooks for your clothes. It was quiet and private.

But Mrs Purvis, now of Eastwoodhill House who joined the Vigilance Committee set up in 1910 to protect these attic dwellers, tells just how 'private' their rooms often were.

> It was quite a thing for the sons of some families to slip up the wee narrow stair. The girls would tell us that if these boys didn't

get their way they would threaten to tell their mistresses that it was the girls made the advances. If they held out, the next thing would be they were out on the street, no pay, no reference, no ticket home.

And Mrs Nell Brodie remembers the set-up well.

There you were, out the door, wi' your wee buckled trunk nowhere to go.

The 'where' they often found was, according to Mrs Purvis, literally the street. With no way at first of getting home, some were drawn willy-nilly into prostitution and later, when they had their takings, too ashamed to face the family, or perhaps afraid that their new-found wealth would dry up when it was found out at home where it was coming from.

The Vigilance people took a house in Glasgow and got someone at the church offices in Edinburgh to contact ministers asking them to send word to the committee when girls were coming to service in Glasgow. Then they helped them to get decent places and set up a centre where they could come for help if they needed it.

Not all the girls felt the need of the Vigilance, and one who could apparently wither a would-be seducer without help remembers . . .

One or two places I had, when I was young and maybe quite bonnie, where the young gent would try you on. As often's not they were just wee nyaffs or big gomerils you wouldnae've looked at twice. So you just laughed at them and called them 'sonny', but you were best to leave if you could, for you couldnae very well tell.

The maids were as great a mixture of personality as the families. Some were timid and easily brow-beaten, but others were not so mealy-mouthed in the face of insult. Certainly not by 1928.

Once when I was gettin' checked for no' doin' behind a sideboard the mistress says to me, quite nippy, 'You'd shift that furniture if you'd seen a two shill'ny bit there to put in your pocket . . . ' Well see! I just went to the kitchen-hook, put on my hat and coat and marched out. I was that angry. But she came to my house after, and

put me up from nine-shillin' a week to ten, just to get me back . . .
didnae make much difference to me mind. I only got to keep
1s. 6d. anyway, and my granny got the rest. It was the principle but.

Even where a maid might be too mim to protest at a rebuke
like that, there were ways for a girl to bide her time and take an
unsuspected revenge . . . unsuspected, at least, by her mistress.

We had a maid called Effie when I was about twelve. Once when
my parents were away for a weekend and just me and my brother
at home I saw her goin' out to meet her young man and she was
wearing a dress of my mother's. I remember it, clear as clear, a
sort of cherry red. My mother was quite sonsy and the dress was
kind of tight on her, and not very nice. But it was just the very
thing on Effie. I looked to see if it was back in the press the next
morning and so it was. I never told my mother because I thought,
well, if it was who it looked right on, the dress was really Effie's.

Sometimes though, a mistress's clothes became legitimate perks.

One of my ladies wore lovely clothes. I wasnae far off the same
size so I often got a dress or coat off her. So here was me on my
afternoon off trottin' away up the town for high tea wi' a fella, in
my Jaeger or my pricey wee number out Macdonald's.

That maid had obviously another perk in the freedom she enjoyed
on her day out, but there were also mistresses who thought it quite
legitimate to control their girls' off-duty pursuits. Some have the
grace in hindsight to look back at their own effrontery.

In our district in Whitecraigs there was a maids' club in one of the
churches. I didn't encourage our Mollie to go at all. I thought they
would just sit there and drink tea, talk about their ladies, maybe
compare wages and days off and the work they had to do. I thought
they might get ideas. Come to think on it now though, *we* all sat
over our afternoon teas and discussed the maids and their short-
comings at great length . . . we had a nerve really, sure we had?

Not all the girls came from hungry or bleak backgrounds. One
recalled by Mrs Margaret Fotheringham came from a river-
fishing family where certain items that were her daily diet would
have been a treat to many city employers.

Her home was up in Perthshire somewhere on the Tay, and when she came for an interview my mother asked if she had any food fads (fikey eaters were a nuisance in busy households). 'I'm not used to have to take salmon more 'n twice in the week.'

In that fad she was no doubt easily accommodated. At least at the outset of her employment that lass did not seem to grovel for her 'place' and there were others who had good enough conceit of themselves not to be trampled on once they were part of the household. Indeed some maids were quite awesome to the children of homes where they worked.

We sometimes went to the pictures with Sadie our maid. She knew all the film stars, Tyrone Power, Douglas Fairbanks, Bing Crosby. Once she was sent to take me to see Shirley Temple at the pictures. That was at the Waverley Picture House. But at the Elephant just along the street Robert Taylor was showing in *Camille*. We went to see *Camille* and Sadie promised me a clout on the lug if I told. I didn't know what a clout on the lug was, but I had a fair idea. I wouldn't have dared tell my mother anyway about seeing *Camille*, because there was kissing in it.

Free visits to the pictures, Jaeger clothes, private rooms, pleasant women to work for . . . easy to understand long years of service and goodwill there. But ungallant sons, suspicious mistresses, treatment as skivvies, why did they thole those?

I remember our minister getting wind of the bad way some women treated their girls, and him giving them a right good telling-off in a sermon . . . reminded them that their maids were human beings, young girls with feelings and rights of their own.

Maybe they tholed conditions that none would tolerate now, because the alternatives were worse. Being in service in the 1920s and 1930s was a way of life for the daughters of families in country villages, and in mining areas where wasting diseases were rife. A place in a decent house with a clean warm bed and good food meant not only gain for the girl but, at home, one mouth less and one stretch of bed more. To be a little drudge was a small price to pay for a healthy settling, and peace of mind for hard-pressed parents. One mistress remembers,

> Our maid Nettie had three sisters and a brother died of TB in the five years she was with us in the 1930s.

And young Violet Baker had surely no wish to go back east to the children's home where they were trained for domestic service and sent out in the snell days of winter to the shore at Musselburgh to gather sea-coal for stoking the home's fires, in the teeth of a wind searing in from the Forth.

By the 1930s, time was running out for the 'general' who had been such an institution in small households for generations. But if the girls who fetched and carried for the nippy and the nice, the careful and the thowless among mistresses, ever despaired that they were faceless nonentities at their work places, they might be surprised to know how well-remembered they are, and with what affection and laughter.

There was Mary Ferguson, who smashed everything smashable, but could heeshie-baw the girniest wean; and Bridie Ryan who kissed her boyfriends goodnight in full view of the children at their bedroom window; Ruby Tate who liked a wee sherry from the sideboard while setting the dining-room table and was indulged in her 'secret' sin because she was a rare hand with a girdle scone. And there was Wee Lizzie, bow-hurdied and Methody, who ruled the household absolutely on the matter of Sabbath observance. Not even knitting for the soldiers was tolerated, and any such war-work had to be stuffed under the Gardner family cushions when she came ben the room to set 'your teas'.

Lizzie had lingered as maid into the war years, one of the very few left. For by the early days of October 1939 the rest were swept away, as if by landslide. They were in factories and the services, on buses or on the land and, for the time being at least, thought they had found El Dorado.

And their mistresses?

I visited a cousin once, who still had a maid long after anyone else, and I found I had forgotten this gracious living; if that's what you call it to have some other woman whisk away your own dirty dishes from under your nose and remove such mundane things from your very consciousness. I decided I didn't miss it a bit.

4

A PENNY-FARDEN FOR A ONE-INCH LINK

At its peak Glasgow was a city of a million people and, since many of them went to their mort-kists before old age or retirement, it followed that, except during periods of serious recession and in spite of all but the poorest women being firmly thirled to scrubbing board and soup-pot or paying afternoon calls, that population went out to a vast range of occupations . . . far too many to do much more in a chapter than passingly bring to mind a few of them.

Some of the earliest handed-down recollections belong to young Maggie Anderson's childhood in the 1890s and are of her great-grandfather, born about 1780.

> Fine I knew my great-grandfather, for he lived wi' my granny. Him and my grandpa were estate workers to the Earl of Home at The Hirsel, but then the Homes took over the Bothwell Estate . . . early last century that would be, and they both came there to work and took houses just outside of Glasgow. That's where I was reared up.

They were estate-men, that father and son, but most of the childhood memories about grandfathers and great-grandfathers which stretch back into the nineteenth century are, perhaps not surprisingly, concerned with the basic provisions of life . . . clothing, warmth and food. When Mr Alick Murdoch's grandfather was still a young man around the 1850s, he saw the end of handloom weaving in East Kilbride.

He was quite shrewd my grandpa, and he could see he'd be just left high and dry if he waited till the last weaving-shop closed down there, so, before all the other out-of-work weavers came pell-mell to Glasgow, he came and tramped the city streets till he got a place at a power-loom mill in Bridgeton and set up his family in a wee house near the Glasgow Green. There was a lot of power-mills in Glasgow by then.

But before they could weave their cloth, there was the spinning, and that was an attic piece-work job done in the workers' own homes. Another grandfather passed on word of that grim life to his family:

Grandpa used to tell me that when he was wee, maybe five years old, his mother used to tease out the wool on pin boards, then spin the yarn on her wheel. It was set up in their single room, all smelly and oosey wi' the wool, and his job was to run between his mother and the mill, wi' creels of wool and pirns, and wi' a tally card to get marked up wi' the week's one-and-sixpenny earnings for her long hours in that attic.

There was the cotton printing too, long ago established at various printfields in Glasgow and employing thousands of workers.

My faither was a labourer in what they called the 'calico' at Thorney-bank. I mind I used to lie in my bed and listen to the voices of the other men comin' up the street, on their way to work by six o'clock in the morning. They used to shout him and other two workers down for the two-mile walk away along the dark road to the printwork for their eighteen shillin' a week.

'You right Jimmy?'
'You right Tam?'
'You right Johnny?'
        and the answers used to come . . .
'Right y'are.'
'Comin'.'
'Just be there.'

After the spinning and the weaving and maybe the printing, there were those who made up the stuffs.

My great-uncle was a master-tailor near Glasgow Cross with a workroom in his house there. You went up an outside stair and pulled a bell that jangled the whole place. And inside, there was my uncle sitting up cross-legged on his big work-bench where he could look out over London Road. It always sticks in my mind that he took £3 for a suit.

You might think that child's memory was misted by fairy-tale. Cross-legged tailors surely belong to Grimm and Andersen and Beatrix Potter; but no less than four rememberers with tailor kin spoke of that traditional bench-squat. 'My uncle? Oh aye, always.' 'My father never worked any other way.' 'It was just the tailors' way . . . my auntie was a dressmaker and she'd just her chair and table.'

So the Glaswegian of the nineteenth century was clad and bedded, to a great extent, in the home-spuns and prints worked by fellow citizens. What about their warmth and nourishment?

Of those whose darg was to keep the home fires burning, many still have recollections of old-time links with those jobs . . . of walking above-ground near the Giffnock railway bridge and hearing miners singing at their work below . . . of the colliers' rows near Cardowan and Thornliebank, of coalmen shouting their wares at 2s. 3d. a bag.

And Margaret Henderson's father is remembered as a tradesman fitting fireplaces for the coal to burn, once it had been gouged out, bought and bunkered.

When I was young in the 1890s my father's work was putting in ranges to folks' kitchens. Ranges were the latest thing after the exhibition . . . must have been the 1888 exhibition . . . anyway it was Bows of High Street that sold them . . . oh aye, he put in a lot of ranges for the Bows' Emporium.

As for food, Glasgow has always provided a fair variety of its own; from the flour mills out at the Bun House that became the Kelvin Hall, from the tea blenders and fruit growers, and even small city farms.

When I lived in Wodrow Street there were still wee farms and holdings, cheek-by-jowl wi' the tenements and mills.

There were butchers and bakers and black-pudding makers, and it was certainly not only menfolk who were masters of such crafts. Mrs Janet Purvis recalls two black-pudding-maker persons. Her mother-in-law and her sister were two young girls orphaned by a train crash as children.

> The girls began work in a lace factory but Mary was quite pushy and they opened their own dairy business with a comfy wee home through the back. They were next door to a butcher and he gave them his scraps and the blood to make black-puddings that he could sell. They became quite expert at it, but they'd one strict rule. They only ever ate the burst ones for their own teas, for they'd have lost their profits eating a good one.

The city even had its very early fast food and Mr Duncan White talks about a one-time Glasgow character called Pie Nanny, whose pitch was at the north end of the Suspension Bridge where she sold pies and pancakes.

> If you wanted yours hot, you ordered it, then went for a walk while she het it by holding it in next to her, inside her bodice under her shawl.

Duncan White doesn't claim to have sampled one of Nanny's long-ago pies . . . but then it was perhaps *belief* that should have been suspended at the bridge.

So much for the work of turning out basic needs. But of course much of the daily work in those boom days of the nineteenth century related to the heavy throbbing industry that was Glasgow's heartbeat. Miss Marie Condie was born in 1896 and remembers one of the hazards of her father's work.

> At that time he was a big-paid man in Colvilles' working with the molten metal as it came out the red hot furnace. But he got rosacea of the skin with that and he'd to give up and go on to selling and installing coal-cutting machines.

And Mrs Muriel Lillie's father was also in iron and steel.

> He used to hoof it all around the country blacksmiths, selling horse shoes and things like that, from his catalogue. Another thing he was

into was the rubber clogs for drivers to put over their horses' shoes to give them a grip, going up cobbly slopes the like of West Nile Street. Goloshes for horses really . . . big sales there were for rubber clogs.

Jim Lillie's father too, travelled to all airts and pairts with his merchandise.

He was in oilskins, and he'd a big basket of samples to trail about with him. So when he got off the train some-place, he used to hire a 'boy' for the day to wheel his hamper on a barrow round his calls and stay outside to keep an eye on it. They'd quite fair wee businesses these barrow boys.

But not everyone toiled at the serious business of prospering and sustaining the city. There were those who beautified and entertained.

My auntie that I stayed with was a hairdresser and done the Marcel wavin' for a shillin' . . . you got a re-set at sixpence . . . d'you mind the Marcel waving?

My mother was a workin' lassie before she was wed, but she learned herself to play the piano by ear, and she must've been pretty good for she played the music at the pictures. She did it all slow when it was love-scenes and fast when it was maybe a chase, then changed it to cloppin' and galumphin' music when Tom Mix was ridin' in a cowboy bit. And then some nights she sang at the piano in a wee tearoom cafe on the road to Paisley, at Spiersbridge.

A last view of the previous generations' world of work comes from Mr James Wisner who remembers old days in Thornliebank.

There was a sort of division among the folks down our way. Nearly everyone was in the print-works right enough, but one lot was just the workers and the other lot was the bosses. They had different houses in different streets. The workers were in the wee rows and the toffs were in Lum Hat Street. And the 'row' weans got chased out Lum Hat Street if they went there to play.

He doesn't add what happened to the small Lum Hat fry when they ventured into the rows.

After these second-hand memories, recollections from the early years of the century are of rememberers' own working days. Some can still see themselves as office boys in bowler hats, apprentices in short trousers, factory girls in overalls and dust caps, shop girls in black dresses and young typists earning six shillings a week where they stood at desks to work.

> Then you understand of course, there were no first names in the office, always Mister and Miss This or That. I even called my best friend Miss Briggs, and for years after we left the office she was still Miss Briggs to me.

One who was an apprentice in those early days before the First World War was William Stevenson.

> I was apprenticed as a joiner to wee Humphy-backit McWhirter the builder. He was close-fisted even then right enough, but I was young and didnae notice . . . and I was getting on fine. But then the war came before I was done and I was away till I was twenty-four, with the hospital and that. I went back to Mr McWhirter and at the end of the first week he handed me a pound for wages . . . a wee apprentice's pay and there's me been a sergeant-major in the Army! But then he got a flea in his lug from the ex-service association and after months of hummin' and hawin' he gave me the right money . . . two-thirds a journeyman pay for ex-servicemen. When I was finished I set up a wee joinery business and did quite nice.

Another who started to his trade before that war was Duncan White.

> I was wi' a railway-wagon shop . . . 'The Slaughter House' we called it, for the sweated labour it was. I made couplin' safety-chains. It was piece work and you got a penny-farden (an *old* penny-farden) for an inch link and out of that you paid your mate. That was your hammerman like. You stood sideways to the fire, in front of your anvil, your feet in a hollow in the ground to keep your exact place. You wore your apron to the side for the heat of the fire, then you bent and skeffed the wee metal bars . . . after that bang! bang! wi' your hammer to close the links tight. You kind of swivelled at your hips to get the rhythm, swingin' between the fire and the anvil . . . it was rare practice for the dancing.

By then, young women in most social groups were persuading their papas that there was more to life than embroidery and making paper flowers, and that they were not beyond redemption simply because they took paid employment.

> I went to work at fourteen with William Collins the publishers in Cathedral Street and I was there until I retired. I worked at the costing of materials, judging the amount of thread and card for making the good stitched books.

The stores were a happy hunting ground for young ladies who fancied meeting the public and working with merchandise they could never have afforded themselves. May Reid was one of those.

> I went into Fraser's at about sixteen. It was old Mr Hugh then, the second one of the four Hughs, and very nice and polite he was . . . came round every day to say good morning and ask after everyone. I mind once I stayed late sorting through a big order of gowns (mantles we called them then) and hanging them up. The caretaker told Mr Hugh and next pay day when he came round with the packets he gave me ten pounds out of his own pocket. TEN POUNDS, I couldn't credit it. But after work I hurried away down to Manson's (yon dear sweetie-shop in St Enoch Square) and bought my mother a half-pound box of chocolates . . . Manson's chocolates!
>
> Through time young Hugh left school and came in to learn the business (him that was Lord Fraser after). He did some of the buying with me . . . nice man, young Mr Hugh.

Another young lady whose mother made sure she went into lady-like employment was Miss Helen Edgar.

> There were lots of works near us, bleachers and dyers and bakeries but my mother wanted us all in genteel jobs, floristry, clerkin' an' that, and one brother was a compositor. Anyway when it was me to leave school she took me straight away down Cogan Street to the mill. She knew the boss-man there.
>
> 'I've brought you a new weaver . . . I don't want her an ordinary weaver . . . she's to be a Madras weaver,' says my

mother. Seven-and-six I got a week while I learned. Then it was piece work at six-and-eightpence for forty yards on my broad-loom, less on my narrow one. When you were skilled you had your two looms, you see, with your web and weft and the punched cards to give you your design.

In the morning you got a mug of tea at your loom but you darenae stop it for you tried to get six pieces made in the week. You didnae manage that often mind, because you'd to stop a lot for the coom (that was the sooty oose that hung about the ceiling) used to fall on your web and jigger the shuttle so's you got dirty wee tears . . . 'scob flaws' they called them and you'd to stop and mark the place, to mend it when it came off the loom. Sometimes there was a breakdown and the tenter had to come and sort it. If he was slow or had a staw at you, and kep' you waiting, that was all lost money. But it was quite a good pay if you worked hard and I took home more to my mother than my faither did. I got 1s. 6d. a week to myself.

Private nefarious schemes, for raising take-home pay unofficially, are no doubt as ancient as the first short-change on bartered fig-leaves, and were as well known in the years just after the First World War as before or since.

> I was in a factor's office when I came back from the war and there was an old twister there who ran his own wee racket; taking key money when folk were desperate for houses to rent. The boss Willie Ross caught him and he got his jotters . . . mind Willie himself wasnae always the clean potato. He got drummed out of the Army for drinking and fighting!

There was consternation from the other party to the interview, startled at this revelation after seventy years, about a Glasgow business man, of old and respected acquaintance. 'Willie Ross did . . . never!' 'Aye he did!' 'Oh my!' says the deflated lady of eighty-seven.

Although many single girls were taking jobs by the out-break of the First World War, those four years confirmed them as a real part of the workforce. Some came back to ordinary occupations from munitions, some from the services. One of them confesses to having been a little confused.

> When I came back from the services I used to forget where I was and stand to attention when I was called to see the boss!

There were post-war adjustments for men to make too, when they found their offices full of women doing very nicely thank you, at almost the whole range of jobs. The men weren't always too diplomatic about reintegrating and some began to throw their weight about 'something awful'. Lists of petty rules began to appear in a number of offices.

> I mind some of the silly orders that our men dreamed up. Daft they were. Here's one I mind. 'No exception will be taken to one signet ring and a watch-bracelet. No more jewellery than that will be permitted.' And this, 'dark clothing only, will be worn at all times under regulation overalls'. Then, because we were 'office', we weren't to hob-nob with 'warehouse'. *You* could call *them* by their first names, by way of work, but they had to call us Mister and Miss. Staff and warehouse were different species of being.

Between the wars there was seasonal work too, and sometimes there were temporary jobs. The Empire Exhibition of 1938 gave work to attendants, clerks, typists, cashiers, building squads, truck drivers and waitresses.

> I worked in the Big Orange. It was a juice stall and it was like a big split-open orange. That split part was your counter and you served there. After that I worked at a stall where they sold hot crisps wi' salt 'n' vinegar in wee paper pokes wi' twirly ends.

From the earliest days there has always been a vast Army of women who clean up when office, factory and warehouse close for the night . . . or serve food to workers while they are there.

> I worked at the cleaning and in the canteens at some of the newspaper offices. I liked the *Herald* best. They used to call me the 'Auld Yin' there. I peeled the veg and tatties and cleaned up the dirty pots and the greasy dishes. Then when the floor got scrubbed you used to get the big-big rolls of newsprint and let it

unwind out, right the length of the canteen floor, so's folk could walk on it wi'out slipping. It was quite interesting workin' there, for when the big news came we got it first. Then the canteen would be open all night and we took round hot soup and rolls.

Some of the rememberers loved their work, some hated it, some tholed it. But whatever the talk of job satisfaction or drudgery, the main interest and gauge of status (though not the only one) was the pay packet; and every last one of them could say just exactly what he or she earned at various stages of working life. 'In 1905 . . . six shillings a week as a photographer's assistant.' '1912 that would be . . . seven shillings as an office typist'. '1920, passing rich on forty pounds, as a bank trainee.' '1930 . . . ten shillings a week when I was a boy workin' to a leather merchant.' '1947, I got twenty pounds a month as a newly qualified teacher.'

And of course there was that 'penny-farden for an inch link' in the first years of the century.

They recall, not only what they earned, but what happened to it and the social consequences of how it was handled.

Although women werenae what you'd say liberated, they really wore the breeks (I'm speaking about the days when it wasnae so much the done thing for married women to be out workin'). My faither wouldnae dared to open his pay packet before he got it home. My mother was real strong. When a man interfered wi' his pay to fritter it, or if the woman was feart for him, she'd a bad time wi' money and the family kind of floundered.

A sad fact borne out by one hard-pressed wife who did not handle the money.

I never saw my man's pay poke till he died sudden and I got the one he was owed. When I saw the good wage he'd really earned, I couldnae believe it. I gret. I'd worked at house-cleanin' all my days just to keep things going.

Booms, recessions, head-work and hand-work . . . Glasgow folk have come through them all with a host of vivid pictures of their jobs, and wry comments on tasks and task masters. And the pawky Glasgow tradition is still alive with young people who are lucky enough to have jobs now; who know they are lucky, but still have the spirit to negotiate their perks.

> My brother's learnin' to be a butcher. He gets to bring home a' the sausages he makes for the first six months till he learns to do it right. I mean, you cannae sell squinty and shapeless sausages over the counter, can you? . . . My mother's hopin' he learns to cut the sirloin steaks wrong an' all.

5

WAGES FOR PRINCIPLE

They've always been a disputatious lot the Scots; since the Middle Ages certainly about their religion, their kings and their land. But later, when working men first discovered how to face up to their 'betters', both sides had whole new worlds for their cantankers. There were a number of centres of unrest all over Scotland, where men chewed the fat about conditions of unemployment and, even more seriously, about conditions of employment. Nowhere was it chewed more vigorously than in Glasgow, with its concentration of industry and the conflicting interests of master and man.

The reek of revolution was in the Glasgow air of the 1820s. Dissatisfaction had been at the simmer for a long time but when mass production came to the mills and began to throw hand-loom weavers out of work, it boiled over.

> There was a tradition in our family of being in the thick of the demands for reform. My grandfather came of radical folk, for they were weaver people and he used to tell me what he minded of those days himself and what he'd been told by his father. His own first home was just the single room with his weaving-loom in the middle and what wee bit else they had, lying round it. The weaving folk had the name of being well-read and booky, for they were self-employed and they could work double time the one day to get reading the radical weeklies when they came out the next.

This grandfather wrote in his journal of seeing workmen meeting together round the doors of thatched cottages in the east end, to listen, while one who could read took the *Penny Post* or the *North British Daily Mail* and read aloud to the rest.

'Where there was weavin' there was agitatin',' my grandpa used to say. 'The government was afraid of revolt.' (This was about the 1820s and it wasn't so long after the French Revolution.) 'They used to put spies in the pubs so's they could listen in, then go and clype on the trouble makers. One got vitriol thrown in his face for being found by the weavers doin' that. Lost both his eyes.' My grandfather used to tell us, as well, how his father was with John Baird and Andrew Hardie the Glasgow Radicals when they got executed at Stirling in 1820, and how he was with Willie Goldie when he got killed in the riot the Scots Guards came to put down.

But the Reform Acts were passed, real revolution did not come and nobody else's grandfather had quite such bloodthirsty 'peacetime' memories. Mr Alexander Murdoch, now ninety-five, remembers,

My grandfather was a great Liberal . . . thought the world of Gladstone. But he parted company with him over the head of Irish Home Rule . . . couldnae thole that idea at all. But he couldnae think to join the Tories either. He was never a Tory. So he took up with the Chamberlains in the Liberal Unionists. I mind of seeing Gladstone myself a time or two in Glasgow at meetings. Very, very popular he was . . . crowds every-where. (They only do that for the queen now, or singers with guitars.) Anyway I was a grown lad when Gladstone died about 1898 or 1899, and I mind that day because the *Glasgow Herald* had thick black borders round it.

Politicians were the popular idols of Victorian times and two people tell the same hand-me-down tale of the reformer John Bright.

John Bright was a great one to a lot of folk, but he lost a wee bit of his popularity when he was so far ben wi' Abraham Lincoln over the slaves an' that. And my father told me, 'Abraham Lincoln wasnae that popular here till after he got shot, then all of a sudden he was a hero.' Glasgow folk liked a good martyr.

As a Lincoln man then, John Bright was back in favour and had the prodigal's rousing welcome when he came to Glasgow. That visit is recorded in the Freer family annals.

My grandfather and his friends that favoured reform wanted to give him a presentation. They thought on a nice inscribed Bible but they couldnae get near him . . . not in the street and not into his hotel. So they strung it on a long bit string across Argyle Street from one-up houses each side, and lowered it into his carriage when it came along.

But it wasn't only the menfolk among the famous reformers that came to Glasgow and its surroundings, and the lady who was little May Gilmour near the turn of the century remembers an unusual setting for a nationally kent figure to be giving her spiel, this time on votes for women.

It was a funny place right enough for Sylvia Pankhurst to be speaking. We used to go on holiday down the Clyde and up to Whistlefield. I was just a wee thing there that year when we heard she was coming to speak. Mind there's nothing at Whistlefield, why she ever came there I don't know, except maybe they wouldn't give her a hall in the city. It meant nothing to me at that age, but it was a holiday ploy and all the visitors and the locals sat on the grassy slope and listened to her there. She was lovely and I mind all the grown-ups saying she was a rare speaker.

Although the suffragettes roused passionate controversy in Glasgow, a booking was allowed for a rally at St Andrew's Halls. But before the day of the meeting Mrs Pankhurst had become their leader . . . she was militant and forthright and thought likely to cause trouble so the manager of the halls was instructed that on no account was Mrs Pankhurst to be allowed to attend that meeting.

It was my grandpa that was in charge, and mind you he was quite a supporter of the women, but he had his orders. They put 100 policemen in the basement and had them on duty all along the roads leading to the halls. Seems ridiculous now but she really had them in a right panic.

Anyway somehow she gave them all the slip and when the rally started she suddenly just bobbed up from behind the table.

The police stormed the platform and there was just a donnybrook wi' the Pankhurst folk and the bobbies. The police had their batons right enough, but here so had the women and *they* didnae know who was for them and who not. So they all just let fly. One of them was getting arrested and in the mayhem she tore my grandfather's coat-tail away, but then she swiped at him with her baton and he grabbed it . . . fair exchange I suppose, the baton for the coat-tail.

Whether the coat-tail has been cherished and handed down in the Pankhurst family or not, Thomas Clydesdale Watson has no idea, but the baton, shown with great pride, has been a treasured trophy in his family since the day Grandpa jouked its swipe.

The heroes who found their land unfit after coming back hopefully from the First World War to the grand promises of politicians, struggled to improve their own lot and serious unrest brought rashes of protest meetings and strikes. Families sacrificed wages for principle, stood their ground and eked out their housekeeping purses in various ways. Daisy Baker remembers her parents' enterprising sidelines.

I mind a strike our way early in the 1920s. My mother made trays and trays of toffee-apples, plain ones and coconut ones, tuppence-a-piece. And my father split sticks and made up wee bundles of them wi' wire. They sold the apples and the firewood at the door to make a wee bit money. She was a rare hand at the toffee-apples my ma.

And the Edgar weans put in their ha'pennyworth to the family kitty.

The pit at Burnfield near Hillpark was out, and us kids were dispatched up there wi' bags to bring back any coals that were lying about. I was just young but even then I could tell coal from slate and just brought home the good stuff.

As the 1920s turned on, social castes were reinforced, and bitter 'them and us' confrontations began to develop. But there were dissent even within the ranks of each side.

I was a very young and frightened lieutenant at the Somme and I fought alongside better men than I would ever be, who came back to houses and wages that were a disgrace. I sometimes couldn't believe that friends of my own who'd been through the trenches with working chaps could be so sore against them in the strikes.

But the scolding of striking workers was not all from the men who had been their officers in France.

I mind when we were in a room-and-kitchen ground floor, and my mother used to bake scones; and here this day, she was standing at the open window doin' a batch of her scones and talkin' out to a wee cluster of striking men standing grumbling on the pavement outside. She started argy-bargying wi' them. I can hear her yet . . . She was a great wee Conservative my mother and she could put by a wee bit of Faither's pay-poke every week.

'I'm a Conservative,' says she to the men.

'Whit've you got to conserve?' says one.

'My bank book.'

'How did *you* get a bank book?'

'Hard work!' says she, and let that sink in while she whisked her scones off the girdle into a towel.

The period's unrest peaked in 1926 with the General Strike, after economics had dictated that miners' wages were to be reduced and hours of work lengthened. Memories of these nine days are vivid to almost all the rememberers. The strike failed to bring workers what they saw as no more than simple justice, largely because there were, by that date, plenty of alternatives to the public transport they tried to paralyse. There was the new wireless too to bring news and entertainment to the public even when the press was silent.

While it was 'on', overlaying the grim determination of the strikers, there was an atmosphere of almost carnival adventure for those who could enjoy the challenge of trying to keep things running with no risk to their own livelihood. Even the weather was bright and sunny.

We were students in 1926 and my pals and I all drove tramcars. You just turned up at one of the tramway depots and maybe an inspector taught you to drive. It was all quite a spree really.

So says one driver. But a passer-by was less sanguine about the quick-taught drivers.

> It was some sight, I can tell you, to see the trams goin' by like trains in India, full inside and up-top, and wi' folk cheek-by-jowl, jammin' the platform, then maybe another dozen hangin' on to the brass pole and the runnin' board. I wouldnae've got on to one for a' the tea in China, I tell you.

Armies of private cars came out like ants from warm woodwork.

> My late husband had business cars and a few horse-drawn carts for local deliveries. He sent them out in the strike to carry people to work. They took maybe ten folk to a car and sixteen or seventeen on the carts.

There was no formal asking or granting of lifts. Non-strikers, without a by-your-leave, simply jumped on and off passing lorries or carts going in the right direction, and 'lapped' their way to work like that on perhaps six different vehicles.

And an unfamiliar Glasgow was revealed to young Isobel Cameron who was a student at Gilmorehill at the time.

> I found all sorts of new ways about the town. I lived in Ibrox and I discovered the ferry. I used to walk along Copland Road on the south side, cross the Clyde and then walk the length of Kelvinhaugh Street at the other end. Great!

For a few days news was posted outside stations and post-offices, an Emergency Press sheet was published and, at the height of the strike, troops were deployed about the city.

> I mind of the soldiers in George Square keepin' order, and that made the men right surly and angry.

Then it was all over. Or was it? They had won nothing and lost much more than just a day or two's wages.

> I was on strike from my work, and after it fell through, everyone at our work wi' under ten years' service got the sack. So I lost my job, for I'd just been working at it since my five years in the Navy in the war. That was seven years I'd worked. They did

that to weed out the younger ring-leaders. A whole generation of workers like, got their books. Anyway I decided to take my family and go to Canada.

So while some, like Duncan White, left Glasgow to look for work after 1926, others, like Janey Brown, hit by the strike and its aftermath elsewhere, came to the city to find new employment.

I came to Glasgow when the depression that came on after the big strike was getting bad. My father'd been a tailor in Manchester with his own place. But there was no more work there, the uniforms he'd made not needed any more, so we came to the Gorbals for him to do his tailorin' for someone else. He worked for a tailor at a place in South Portland Street, in what's now Morrison's.

And for those who like their endings happy the climax of these last two tales of going and coming, is that the travellers met and married much later, he driven home by lack of work in Canada, she, by then, having settled and adopted the city as home.

Real protest can thrive only on some glimmer of hope and even that died when the 1920s closed in slump, so that people became dejected and dispirited. Even bright, well-qualified young people, the grandparents of the 1980s' young unemployed, found it hard to get work.

I trained as a language secretary and it was nearly a year before I found a job. Even then it wasn't what I'd studied for.

Men who had been lads in the First World War and become the angry strikers of 1926, were the disillusioned fathers of families by the early 1930s.

My father was minister in Govan and knew his people well in that parish. Most of the men in his congregation were in the shipyards like Lithgows, and Harland and Wolff, and Stevens of Linthouse, and he was heart-sick for those decent working men with skills going to waste through the slump years.

Sad times, aye. But there's a wee wag to the most glum tales and Mr Joe Kyle has it in a memory of his, linking 1926 and 1939.

In the General Strike I volunteered as a special constable. I was sworn in, very serious, then sent home to wait, all champing at the bit to get into action. And I heard not another word . . . for thirteen years! Never called out once. Then in 1939 I was suddenly sent for and lined up with others to get a long service certificate . . . and given my duties as a wartime special!

It took the Second World War to set the factory machines turning again, the hammers clanging, the cranes swinging in the yards; a heavy price for men to get back their industrial self-respect. Since then, the 1940s', '50s and '60s, the years of the never-so-good life, have passed into memory like the fight for votes, and the old slump. Now the new slump has come. The style of unemployment is different, victims are better buffered against bare want, the job lack cuts a wider social swathe, but the blight to the spirit is just as bitter.

6

LUM HATS AND LEG O' MUTTONS

That photographer who shuttered the family group at the opening of a previous chapter captured not only the clothes of babies and children that we have already remembered, but those of their parents and grandparents as well. So while the young fry skipped and peeried in tammies and sailor suits how did the bien-dressed elders of earliest memory look?

> My father used to tell me that when he started his apprenticeship in the 1880s the senior men came to work in tall hats, black jackets and striped trousers!
>
> I suppose my granny would be about fifty in the 1890s when I mind of her in a bonnet wi' ties under her chin and leg o' mutton sleeves to her dress. It had all embroidery down the front and she'd a shawl wi' that. Then sometimes in the house she'd a wee fuss of lace on the top of her head.

By the early twentieth century bonnets were left to the very old, and bigger hats were 'in'.

> My granny was in her eighties when I was young around 1905, and I can just see her wearing a tied-on bonnet with a peak down her forehead. She wore a pelisse-thing too and she was all in black, but for a wee touch purple on the bonnet.
>
> My mother had a big felt hat wi' a bird and feather to it . . . very flat . . . my brothers used to call it her doo-lander.

That was country style out in Uddingston village, but across the city on the gracious avenues and gardens of Pollokshields ladies took the air in upmarket versions of Mother Harper's doo-lander.

> I remember my mother in a flat cartwheel hat, very shallow with huge roses on the brim. She wore a lacy dress with a stand-up collar that had stiffeners in it.

Contemporary and probably 'ages' with Granny, around 1910 Mr Watson of Redhurst at Williamwood, came in his carriage to the station every morning to take the train into the city. Little May Reid used to peer through her garden railings into the station yard.

> He was *very* stylish in his shammy gloves and his wing collars and with a silver knob to his walking cane.

There are surely no equivalent watersheds now in young lives that have boys and girls trembling one day on the brink of adult hood and taking the plunge right into it the next, such as there were in the teen years of the century . . . watersheds like putting up the hair or letting down the trousers.

> Edith Wallace remembers her ordeal.

> It was usually at eighteen you put your hair up and I mind after a year as just a wee typist wi' my hair long, being that nervous about going into the office wi' mine's piled up and stuck through wi' a comb. But by the end of the week I really thought I was something and got quite sniffy wi' the junior still in her pleats.

And Joe Kyle his.

> I wore short trousers for nearly a year when I was apprenticed at the bank. It was quite a thing to walk in the first time in your longs.

For vast numbers of young adults in the overshadowed 1914–18 war years, clothing was uniformly drab, the men in khaki or blue, the women keeping them sombre company. The only vivid memory of happier fashion is of May Gilmour's honeymoon outfit in 1918. Out comes the photograph of an elegant and beautiful young woman in a classic cream wool belted coat with full skirt, worn with a French priest-style shallow bowler, with wide brim tilted slightly and sweeping round the crown in a great halo . . . a far cry from the days when she wondered if she would never get anything bought.

A far cry too from the style of a remembered governess of the same era.

> You didnae get a lot of governesses in Glasgow, but this one lived near us and she wore wee nipped-in waists and stiff collars. When you went to visit her and her brother, they always used to sing, 'When you and I were young Maggie'. But you couldnae see her young somehow, and fleein' about in a tammy or that!

Perhaps because the great change to the lounge suit was just round the corner, that period of fathers' attire is very well remembered.

> When we used to go for a walk after church just before the First World War, Father wore a frock-coat and his tile hat. I can see him yet, standing there in the hall on a Sunday morning polishing round the pile of that hat with a velvet pad.

And here's the same gentleman in a family group of the time, sure enough, in the rounded collar and high-buttoned waist-coat with a double loop of gold watch chain, aged perhaps sixty, with white walrus moustache and smoothly parted snow-white hair. Other fathers of that period are remembered with just as much affection but differently.

> My father was a workin' chap and I mind that on Saturdays and holiday he wore a big flat skippit bunnet . . . 'doo-landers' they called them caps.

And a certain Mr Wilson who, whatever else he may have achieved in a long life, is remembered by one young neighbour for nothing more than the hat he wore in 1912.

> Not a tall hat, not as high as that . . . half, maybe . . . and stiff, wi' a curly brim.

The tall hat was subsiding a little, at least for middle-management. Certainly by 1917 the gaffers from Lum Hat Street,

Thornliebank, who went out to work now in three-piece suits and spats, had bowlers instead of lums on their heads (only the gaffers, of course, from the local print-work lived in Lum Hat Street).

The best judge of what a Glasgow gent in his prime should have been wearing then was surely Mr Hugh Fraser, grandfather of Sir Hugh of the Green Canopies on the Paisley's building.

> When I first went to work at Frasers' of Buchanan Street, it was old Mr Hugh I was under. He was coming on a bit by then . . . he'd just a wee fringe of white hair. His chauffeur, Milligan, brought him to business at exactly 9.20 every morning and he used to wear a navy Melton coat with an astrakhan collar, and he would be carrying a wee bag. We used to wonder what was in his bag . . . don't think it would be his piece, mind.

And no doo-lander either for the likes of Mr Hugh Fraser.

As more and more women joined the workforce on the way into the 1920s, their clothes became more practical. At the end of the war they were still wearing ankle-length skirts and hand-span waists, but by 1920 stays were out and short loose jackets and straight lines were in.

> I mind my goin'-away clothes in 1923. I had a beigy-colour boxy costume wi' a loose blouse, and I had shoes to match and my first-ever pair of light stockings. I had a pale straw hat wi' flowers to go my honeymoon in too, and a bonny wee cloche hat for wearing when I got there.

Hair was bobbed too and Miss Marie Condie remembers the scissors finally crunching through her twenty-five years' growth, and the sight of it lying round her shoulders and strewn on the floor.

> I was a nurse and you werenae allowed to get your hair cut. So I had the cuttings made into a bun and pinned it under my cap for work. But I was always in a cold sweat for fear the wee tuffety bits would show and I would get dismissed.

By the 1920s and 1930s, Granny too was into the loose-hung look and most men from eighteen to eighty wore lounge suits which, give or take waistcoats, galluses and vents, have little altered in fifty years.

The Second World War-time years plunged happier memories of fashion into the gloom of passed-on clothes, make-do-and-mend and clothing coupons. In time, trends revived and there have been a few discernable styles . . . the long-skirted romantic New Look of the 1950s, the cheeky minis of the 1960s, and the million miles of denim. What look to us like frenzies of short-lived fads may be treasure to fashion archivists of the future. Who knows, for instance, what they'll make of the day of the platform sole? And with this perhaps apocryphal tale we'll leave the fashion of the late twentieth century to them.

> I knew a girl who had a pair of yon big-big high platforms, and here she's comin' along Argyle Street in them one day, clip-cloppin' past a workman sortin' somethin' down a manhole. His head comes pokin' up and he watches the feet comin' by.
>
> 'Haw, how d'you get down off of them, Hen?' says he. She trots on and just calls back disdainfully over her shoulder . . . 'I dreep, son.'

7

DO YOU MIND OF HENGLER'S CIRCUS?

Picnics, sails, fairs, penny-geggies, Saturday 'bursts', recitals, plays, concerts and operas . . . it would have been a poor-spirited Glasgow cratur of the past century and a half who couldn't find a treat or night out to suit his taste and pay-poke.

Most entertainments over the period were regular features of city life, but there were some one-offs, some annuals and there were the big short-term Exhibitions of 1888, 1901, 1911 and 1938.

Memories of the 1888 one with its Oriental theme and its reconstruction of the old Cathedral clergy houses are inevitably second-hand, but its consequences are worth a mention since the money made from it went to the building of the Kelvingrove art galleries.

> My father talked to me a lot about that exhibition for it was the year I was born in 1888. Two things he used to say . . . that Joe Lyons had a big tearoom there with waitresses all dressed up like Mary Queen of Scots, and that it was that Exhibition made Glasgow start to feel proud of itself.

Not many now remember the 1901 Exhibition held in the area of Kelvingrove Park, affectionately called 'The Groveries' for the period, but young Alexander Murdoch was a schoolboy then and a regular patron.

My father had a business stand there and he gave me a season ticket. My, what a sunny summer it was, sun from morn till night . . . I can think back on a wee bridge over the Kelvin with fairy lights . . . and the gondola with two gondoliers they called Hokey and Pokey. But it's the bands I mind best. There was Sousa's band and the Zouave bugles and a big, big concert hall. The buildings had all wee kind of onion domes. It was s'posed to be Spanish but I mind it more Chinese . . . but aye, it's the bands I can hear yet . . . and I mind the big car competitions between the likes of Wolsleys and Daimlers . . . all open cars of course. The art galleries was opened the same day as the Exhibition.

The 1911 extravanganza at Kelvingrove is well within living memory and although the replica of Falkland Palace (which was blown down in a storm the night the Exhibition closed) and the replicas of a typical Scottish town and village are dutifully reported, the recollections that remain most vivid are those of less educational activities.

That was a rare summer. There was a lot of model ships on the river and a wee boat done up in the McBrayne's colours sailing up and down the Kelvin. There was an overhead railway too and the trucks used to roar right down into the park from Lord Roberts' statue in the Park Circus. I mind seeing a truck gettin' stuck halfway . . . and just hingin' there. And I mind the bands that used to play 'Abide with me' every night.

It was the same memory-story in 1938. For all the treasure store of history and geography, art and science, offered in the great pavilions, and doubtless properly appreciated at the time, most visitors confess to having better mindings of hushed groups watching the Stratosphere Girl risking life and limb with her acrobatics performed high up on a swaying pole, the screaming joy of a hurl on the scenic railway, or a jaunt up Tait's Tower . . . and one housemaid of the time admits, with a happy sigh, to having looked for 'fellas' in the amusement park on her days off.

The Exhibition was a Mecca for kings, queens and princesses, and other instantly recognisable greats.

Funny the things that come best to mind. All very interesting it was, but to this day what I remember is, when Gracie Fields arrived to visit the Exhibition and she just stood in front of the crowd, and sang. Not a set performance, just a spontaneous turn. I thought she was splendid. The books all say it was a real wet summer, but I always remember it sunny.

The Exhibitions then were Glasgow 'putting on the style', milestones along the routine years. But between times there were the week-in-week-out looked-forward-to treats that relieved the long hours of hard work most folk remembered of their younger days.

Early on they had what they called Saturday night 'bursts' . . . kind of shillin'y concerts where you got your tea and a bag of cakes. They got that name because after you'd ate your buns an' that, you blew up your bag and bang! You burst it. My father was on the committee to audition the turns and he minded seeing Harry Lauder, and giving him his first chance on the platform at the Bridgeton Town Hall.

About the same time there were more prestigious concerts at the St Andrew's Halls, where instrumentalists like the Albertini Band of Mandolins and Guitars and 'chantatrices' like Jessie McLachlan and Ada Leigh, regularly charmed the faithful. The City Hall performers had their following too, among them, young Nancy Reid.

My friend at school came of a theatrical family that did turns at the Saturday afternoon concerts. Ginny was tiny and she wore a wee suit of gent's evening clothes and went on as the Pocket Vesta Tilley. I nearly bust with pride that she was my friend.

Drama too had its place at the Penny Concerts in the various Corporation Halls.

They used to show plays on Saturday afternoons (now I'm speakin' about 1906 or 1907). There were *Jeanie Deans* and *East Lynne*, and I mind *Rob Roy* an' all. You used to could get in for nothin' and a free programme, halfway through, and pester your neighbours to tell you what happened in the first half.

Then there were the Argyle Street waxworks, the Panopticon and the Animatograph, rounds of the booths at the fair on Vinegar Hill with its coconut shies and hurdy-gurdy music.

An 86-year-old 'does' Vinegar Hill all over again, chuckles and wags a finger at the earnest group pressing for her recollections.

> Och your mother and me and Mary Grady had the time of our lives when we were young.

But upmarket to all these and the local artistes of music-hall and 'burst' before the First World War, were the real concerts, usually in St Andrew's Halls. Tickets were no doubt expensive, but there were open sesames if you knew how to find them . . . one young man heard Caruso sing, by getting the nod from an official towards a ladder leading from a top corridor, and clamping himself to a roof joist.

> . . . that joist fair vibrated when he hit the high notes.

But steeplejacking wasn't the only way to join the audience without paying. You could cling to other things.

> My best friend was a rare pianist. She played sheet music in Paterson's for customers swithering between buying this piece or that, and she used to get free tickets for two for the celebrity concerts. I stuck like a limpet to that friend and bought myself a nice dress that I wore everytime to the St Andrew's Halls. It was always evening dress at big theatres and concerts then.

With the coming of moving pictures a whole new world of entertainment was opened up. Glimpses of incredible American glamour and romance dazzled your average wee Glasgow chap doing his courting with a poke of sweeties and a tuppenny tramride, and his girl, waiting for either him or for her 'china' at a draughty close-mouth, in her other dress and her best scent.

> When we were wee, we used to get a penny to go to the pictures at the Burgh Hall on a Saturday. Took the whole afternoon that did, because you stood queuing from about one, for the three o'clock showing. Then when I was just started work I got a chum, a china. She was very adventurous and opened big doors to me . . . like going to the Savoy picture-house in the town! You'd to queue for about an hour there, under a canopy but we didnae grudge a

minute for there was buskers there. An old man used to sing . . . oh I cannae mind it all, but it began . . .

'Oh if only, oh if only, she would put away her knittin'' . . . ' Just as well I dinnae mind the rest of that. He did wee dances an' all . . . it was just part of Saturdays early in the 1920s . . . the jugglers and paper-tearers and the singers.

The pictures enthralled vast numbers every Saturday night for fifty years, and if you had the inclination, and the 2s. 3d. in your pocket, you could slip in a visit to the repertory theatre mid-week as well. Throughout the 1930s and '40s the Brandon Thomas Company, or the Wilson Barrett, played to faithful audiences enjoying a weekly dollop of drama.

Some outings didn't involve performances at all, tea at Miss Buick's or Miss Cranston's, or at James Craig's (slightly more stodgy in scone-texture and decor but with interesting exhibitions of pictures). For the west end or south side ladies there were afternoons to be dawdled away in the elegance of Rennie Mackintosh's Willow Tearoom, or Copland and Lye's with its trio or quartet of Palm Court musicians.

And there were the kind of shopping trips remembered by Miss Marie Condie from her childhood around 1902.

I went with my grandma to Anderson's Polytechnic for shopping, for clothes and household things an' that. Then we always went to Ferguson's for a pot of tea and a cake . . . I loved that.

Other bairns had grander destinations.

I used to go with my father to see the pictures at Reid and Lefevre the art dealers, at their gallery. Alexander Reid was a friend of his and it was him advised Sir William Burrell about paintings and put him in the way of collecting some of them you see now at the Burrell. He lived with Van Gogh in Paris when they were young and Van Gogh painted yon famous portrait of him. Talked a lot to my father about his days in Paris.

These were the any-day, any-week outings of long ago, but there were other seasonal or annual junketings that you had to wait for, ticking off your calendar week by week till the great day came or the summer sun shone again, for the Sunday school trip, the paddle-steamer down the Clyde; and perhaps best of all, the arrival of Hengler's Circus. They all recall it but Davie Marriott's is the earliest memory.

> I'm goin' back mind, to about 1901, but it came year after year for a long time. There was this big arena wi' clowns and jugglers, acrobats an' that. But the last turn was what you really waited for. Before it started they put up a big high splash-screen all round, with scenery of woods and waterfalls, except at the entrance. Then some way or other the floor sank down and water gushed in, then Indians in canoes came scooshing through, like they were shootin' rapids.

A quiet man interrupts suddenly from a corner of the Eventide home lounge.

> . . . and d'you mind the horses an' all? Like cowboy films? There was maybe just about six injuns on horses but they seemed like a hunner-an-six because they didnae come up again through the water, they went out some underwater way, then round and back up to do the plungin' again and again.

And his friend gave one of Glasgow's winking, sideways nods of sheer pleasure in shared experience.

> Och aye . . . Hengler's . . . aye, aye.

There were the simplest of all pleasures too, picnics in near by fields on summer days . . . no cars, no pâté, no chicken, no chilled wine.

> We'd picnics down Jack's orchard. You'd get your big jug of skim milk to go wi' your piece 'n' jam and teeter away down the field tryin' no' to slop it afore you got sat down under a special big apple tree. Sometimes we played daisy-chains, and sometimes it was shops, wi' stones and leaves and wee windfall apples. Big stones was for tatties.

That was in the 1890s. Picnics weren't new and have never been out of fashion since. Through wars and catastrophes weans have been skipping into city parks or along outskirt burn-paths . . . even into graveyards, with their baskets and unbreakable cups, searching for the best places to set them down.

> We used to go over the kirk hill at Eastwood, two families of us wi' our baskets. I mind one day we met old Lawyer Robertson that lived up Mansewood. We were all rosy and puffed from cavorting about at the picnic, the eight Morrisons and the six of us Edgars, wi' the two mothers.
>
> 'My what bonnie bairns!' says he. 'They're all that alike, how d'you tell the one lot from the other to get them home?'
>
> 'Oh,' says my mother, 'we just coont them an' hauf them.'

Some special picnics were further afield, and part of a bigger gathering, Sunday school or Woman's Guild outings, or some like the one where Captain Peter Laurie has a sharp picture of himself as a small boy in the 1930s.

> I had an uncle who was a pipe major and he once took me down the Clyde to hear his pipe band at the Cowal Games, in Dunoon. There was me, just a wee chap in this great huge field with my picnic and I remember getting this big busby plumped down over my head and it coming right down to my chin.

In the winter, of course, for the halflin' generation, there was 'the dancin'', not to be confused with 'going to dances' or balls, which was altogether more formal and convention-ridden, with long dresses, dinner or tail coats, with cards, wee pencils, white gloves, Mother's blessing, and a quarter at McEwans' ballroom dancin' lessons behind you. 'The dancin'' was not even to be confused with tennis-club hops, Bible class socials or doing the Charleston at twenty-first birthday parties at the Plaza. 'The Dancin'' was ongoing every night of the week, a public pay-your-money and take-the-floor activity, and it was the big time to thousands.

> For a while I went to the dancin' at the Dennistoun Palais every Friday and then for a wee while it was Barrowland . . . just by the Barras . . . But Green's wi' the different big bands like Joe Loss and Geraldo was the really classy place.

But first of course they had to learn the chassés and the quick-quick-slows, and it wasn't everyone who tripped along Sauchiehall Street with their patent pumps to the select McEwans' studio.

> I just went to Thomsons' in Cumberland Street around the time of the First World War where they learned you quadrilles and lancers, and when you were comin' on a bit and gettin' good at it, they put you to fox-trots and so on.

Duncan White took his dancin' seriously, with almost missionary zeal.

> I mind much later, maybe twenty-five years after, we were living in a house that had a long stretch of grass to the front and I showed a friend how to do that fox-trot I'd learned at Thomsons' . . . a walk first, then seven wee trots and a long scooshy glide . . . that was a long time after. I used to go jiggin' at the Dixon Hall too. I was a keen dancer so I was.

And a short demonstration follows from a man who served all through the First World War seventy-five years ago.

Another who didn't go in for the white gloves and programme-card was Rose Baker.

> Did you ever hear of the Spookies at Gorbals Cross?

We hazard a guess . . . ghost films, or some dark maze of back-courts and dunnies? . . . Back-street waxworks?

> Naw! The Spookies was the spiritualists. We used to go there just for devilment. I went wi' my pal and they used to have you holdin' hands and feelin' for vibrations or some such. Anyway after the meetin' was done you used to hang about and have a wee dance to the piano in the corner that someone could tinkle a bit. But here one night the hall got raided by the police and we got caught.
>
> 'Yer name?' the polis wanted to know.
>
> I had to appear at Craigie Street station.
>
> 'What were you doin' there?' says the man.
>
> I was scared to tell about the Spookies so I says, 'Was there for the dancin',' but that was daft of me, for the place was nae licensed for dancin' and I got fined two bob.

Glasgow was dancing-daft for the first half of this century and while there was something of the mating ritual about it, many a fox-trotter paid his money for sheer love of the dancing.

> I loved all kinds, and I didnae care if there wasnae enough men. I just done it wi' my china. We went to the Sequin Dancin' at a hall in Govanhill. It was that popular that I mind of a friend tellin' me about the long waiting list to join. She says a woman went to put her name down and the girl at the desk says, 'There's sixty-odd name doon to start next week a'ready Hen.'
>
> So this woman just nods at the baby she's got in her arms, 'Aweel,' she says, 'if your list's that long and you'll no' take my name, just put her'n doon instead.'
>
> Och your mother and me an' Mary Grady had the time of their lives when we were young. And so did you and your pals . . .

And so will your granddaughter and my granddaughter and some other Mary Grady . . . if the yen for music and movement, picnics and entertainers still remains the Glasgow characteristic it's been for generations past.

8

THERE WAS A SLITTER IN EVERY CLOSE

Weans who lived up closes in the days when they expected a clout for misbehaviour did not much notice whose hand it came from. The close was a tight-knit community and neighbour-mothers doled out their cuffs evenhandedly to their own and other villains; whatever mother was witness delivered the slap or scolding to whatever culprit was caught.

> I had a pal that lived in a house wi' a garden, and I mind once he came to our close to play at dropping wee bags of builder's sand from the top landing into the dunny. Mistress Waddell down-the-stair (her that we called Ducky-toddle) came out and took her hand off the side of myhead. My pal was mesmerised.
>
> 'Are you no' goin' to tell yer ma on her?' says he.
>
> 'An' get another fae her? No fears,' says I, 'not on yer Nellie!'

Always a common entry for the inhabitants of the block of houses, until the Second World War the close was also a thoroughfare for delivery and other traffic. Postmen brought letters that all the neighbours knew about, even before they fell through the right letter box. Message-boys puffed up the stairs with great baskets of groceries on their heads, carrying dawds of butter spaded-out from big slabs behind shop counters, steeping-peas for soup, sugar and soaps and sodas, Belfast ham, lorne sausage and mouse-trap cheese. Tinkers came, selling clothes-pegs and looking for pieces for the peely-wally offspring happed in their shawls. Milk-boys clattered and whistled, up and down, carrying maybe a dozen long-handled milk-cans over each arm. In hoity-toity closes even newspapers were delivered.

As well as the communal rearing of bairns and the general traipsing in and out of dwellers and those who called on them, pride in the close was common to all (or almost all) . . . the tiled walls of the upmarket wally entries kept washed and shining, the plain plastered ones well-scrubbed and whitewashed.

The sedate colours of the tiles in 'good' closes were ornament enough, but the hoi-poloi kept upsides with the bien by decorating the floors of their entries at the wall edges with pipeclay scrolls carefully and precisely applied in designs peculiar to each close . . . and on the matter of the white-clay handiwork, woe betide the slattern who let the others down! As William Stevenson remembers . . .

> There was a slitter in every close didnae do her pipe-clayin' right, and splashed the walls when it was her turn to wash the entry and the stair. We'd one like that and there was a right bit of aggrava-tion over her, I can tell you. The rest didnae get on with her at all. And it wasnae just the untidy whitenin', she left Brasso smudges round the wee knobs down the banister an' all.

Another who risked the rough edge of maybe eighteen tongues was the coalman who tramped dirty boots all the way to a three or four-up bunker, leaving a trail of black dust behind him. Of course there were some who forestalled that calamity with a sheet of newspaper on every step of the stair.

A quick shifty up your average Glasgow close now suggests mutual tolerance, to the point of coma, of dull brasses, un-brushed floors, wind-swept litter and grimy landing windows. And out beyond the dunny, back-courts are silent wastelands (except where they are expensively grant-landscaped) and empty of all but a woman here and there, on her day off, hanging out clothes on her neat new whirly.

But in earlier days back-courts were colourful arenas of adventure, entertainment and the search for treasure. Weans played there, and wash-house roofs and coal cellars, fences and barred windows were of the very stuff of tigs and hets and hide-'n'-seeks.

> Wherever you were going or whatever you were doin' when you were young, you met your pals there, but what I liked best was the back green singers. There was a partic'lar kind of back-court voice as if the singers were half throttled and they used to kind of slide up 'n' down the notes,

and no Glaswegian over fifty, who hears it said of a singer that he has a back-court voice, needs to have it further analysed.

> They sang under the windows, maybe a man or woman alone, maybe a couple. It was usually Irish songs, like the 'Rose of Tralee' or 'Danny Boy'. If your ma thought they were really down in their luck she used to throw over a penny or two in a poke. If she thought they'd make straight for the pub wi' that, then it would just be a jammy piece.

Two entertainers remembered by Mr James McClelland were the envy and delight of the weans in Silvergrove Street in the 1920s.

> One had a windy-up gramophone he hurled round in a pram, and he sang and danced to that. Another one I mind had a dressed-up monkey and a hurdy-gurdy.

Then there were the troupes of unwitting entertainers who came after dark and rummaged in the bins.

> We used to stand at the window and watch the midgey-men wi' their torches or their candles, late at night, rakin' through the rubbish tryin' to find somethin' worth takin'. I cannae think *what* though, for never a thing went out of most houses that was worth a brass bawbee.

Perhaps the only one likely to throw away carelessly would be the shiftless outsider woman who slittered the stairs and was lax with her chalk squiggles. There must have been prodigal wasters though or the midden rake wouldn't have been worth the candle.

Nancy Wall remembers her first encounter with a midgey-man when she was about twelve, in the 1920s.

> We'd just flitted to this house from a cottage outside Glasgow. It was the winter and dark, and I was sent down the back one night to put the wringer in the wash-house, for the morning. I did that, and then just when I was goin' to lock the door there was this awful loud bash an' bangin' right beside me and I could see a man at the bins wi' a light. I dropped the key and ran for dear life up the stair and I got a right good flytin' for leavin' the wringer there for the man to take or, worse even, give him a shelter for the night. But flytin' or no, I wouldnae go back down there for nob'dy, and my faither had to go and lock the wringer in safe.

So the tenement precincts had their drifting population of performers and errand-boys, scaffies and hawkers; and in biener areas where they spurned the pipe-clay as 'common', there were paid stair-wash ladies like poor Woodbine Annie who roamed the Pollokshields closes forty years ago with her bucket and was said to be skuddy-naked under the long coat she wore to her ankles.

But the best-loved caller of all was surely the lamplighter.

> In the winter when you came home from the school and it was gettin' dark, you used to dawdle in the street for fear the close was all ghoulie and dark. Then you used to see the learie goin' into the close and run to watch him pokelin' up his flame-stick to the gas mantle and yon sort of greenish light comin' sputterin' and floodin' the close and chasin' away the shadows. And then it was safe to go up the stair.

Nightfall still brings its own distinctive feel to the tenement world and where day has held the cheerful bustle of pram manoeuvring and doorstep clash, children at play and the traffic of daily work, all less now but to be found here and there even yet; only the earnest whispering of courting couples, quick passing shadows and echoing footsteps people the closes and dunnies after dark.

9

LOOKING FOR A CLICK

When I was going out with my young man in the 1950s he took me to visit an old man he knew, a Mr Draper.

'So you're winching at last are you Erchie?' says he and he looks me up and down with never even a how d'you do. I was black-affronted I can tell you, and if I'd thought for a minute that what my attentive and romantic Archie was doing was anything so vulgar as 'winching' it would have been all off, there and then.

So says Margaret Pollok of Riddrie. Maybe she had an early, liberated distaste for the idea that it was all his doing and she was just a hapless victim.

I thought we were just modestly getting to know each other and if we both liked what we found, we'd take one another.

Well, maybe some did it old Mr Draper's 'rough wooing' way and others Margaret Pollok's genteel exploration way, but whatever was the truth about Erchie's attitude, there's always been plenty of *it* going on.

I was in service (och, this would be round about the 1930s) early on . . . it was a big house in Jordanhill. They had a cook an' all, a Mistress Good, and I had to help a bit in the kitchen as well's being the housemaid.

The milkman used to come in every morning wi' the milk and the rolls and the pat of fresh butter for their high teas. I was always put to gettin' the milkman a cuppa tea. I was just about sixteen and he never looked the road I was on . . . just sat there, right gallus, tellin' his funnies to Mistress Good.

Then after maybe eighteen month, here I'm washin' the back step one day when he comes out and he says to me,

'This yer hauf-day Hen?'

'Aye.'

'D'you fancy the pictures . . . Laurel and Hardy?'

'Y'askin' me?'

'Three o'clock then, the park gate,' says he and away he goes to his cart.

Well he slep' all through that picture, *Fraternally Yours* I always mind it was called. I didnae know what 'fraternally' meant or I would have thought it was just like the thing that day . . . me sittin' eatin' the sweeties and him gruntin' away beside me.

Anyway I think it would be just maybe the twice more we goes to the pictures, and then he comes in one mornin', puts the bottles on the table, while Mrs Good was in the pantry at the back.

'D'you tell her we're gettin' wed? says he, quite jokoh.

Says I, 'Dod Clark I hardly know you.'

'You're a blether. I'm sure I've been in an' oot here since-ever you came. D'you think I fancied her?'

'No, I think you fancy yoursel',' says I.

Anyway Mrs Good thought a lot of him for bein' a steady and reliable sort of chap, and I took him.

Courtship wasn't always so direct, and sometimes there were real obstacles in the way. Mr A.B. Murdoch remembers hearing of his father's problems over the lady he called Miss Right. When the young James Murdoch went for a weekend down the Clyde to Hunter's Quay in the 1870s, two things happened. He met Miss Alice Brown and he heard the Free Kirk minister preach at Dunoon. He came back home to Glasgow saying, as a serious-minded man should, that he had been very taken with the Free Kirk minister.

But the funny thing was, it was the charms of Miss Alice that lingered longer in his memory. She was the daughter of the wealthy Mr Brown, business man and power in the community at Hunter's Quay. So James' problem was that as a young man starting out in a small way of trade himself, and living in a modest cottage at Tollcross, he felt he was in no position to pay his respects to the bonnie Miss Brown. She had won his heart, but not his head or his pride.

My father couldnae bring himself to court her and thought, how could the likes of him think to win the likes of her? But here a year or so later the thing that was calamity for half of Glasgow was his chance. The City Bank collapsed and my father heard talk that Mr Brown had lost about everything in that crash. Well . . . after that he was up and down to Hunter's Quay every chance he had, and by the spring of the next year, before her father's affairs had picked up again, Miss Alice was Mistress Murdoch, quite happy and content in the cottage at Tollcross.

Fathers loomed quite large in courtships of earlier days. They were jealous of their daughters' welfare, and not so helpless to ensure it as they are now. They had authority and they asserted their rights. Mrs Margaret Henderson was married in 1916, but she recalls a much earlier romance . . . with another dairyman-Romeo.

The soor-dook man was courting me. D'you mind the soor-dook carts? Soor-dook was the left-overs when the dairy-wife was done makin' the butter . . . buttermilk it was really. Anyway I liked yon chap and he liked me, and we used to go into the town for our high teas sometimes. I mind too that he bought me the first pair of fur-back gloves I ever had. He wanted me to marry him and go off wi' him to Canada.

'You're no' gaun near Canada,' says my father. And that was that. You obeyed your father in those days. So I didnae get to marry the man wi' the soor-dook cart. I just thought to mysel', 'Well it's no to be, Maggie-girl, it's no' to be.' But I liked him fine mind.

Another pursuit that hadn't a hope of ending in marriage was that by a kilted soldier of the girl in the fishmonger's shop around the time of the First World War. He was stationed in Glasgow and his duties, or his inclinations, took him past where she worked every day. 'It's a fishy tale this,' says her granddaughter Norma Smith.

This soldier took a notion to my granny. She was a lassie workin' in a fresh-fish shop near the market and every mornin' when she was standin' there guttin' the fish he would come by and plague the life out of her to go out with him. And he used to lean over where she was slittin' and cleanin' the fish, him thinkin' himself a fine catch in his kilt and that. She used to get that mad, my

granny, when he came swingin' along and turned in to pester her.
So one day when he was at his usual, standin' there keepin' her off
her work, she just wheeched up his kilt and slapped him on the
buttocks wi' a cod!

That codswallop was delivered within fifteen years of the deco-
rous Victorian days, when only the heedless broke the rules of
decent behaviour between man and maid. There were other
signs too of fresh winds blowing, although parents were still
strict, and certainly to be overtly obeyed.

For instance there was a kind of street-walking enjoyed by
streams of youths and girls, who became the quite awesomely
responsible Glasgow citizens of later years. But in their greenstick
days they paraded along certain areas of the city most notably
on Great Western Road and around Kelvingrove art galleries on
the north side of the river, and Victoria Road on the south.

> That paradin' up and down Vicky Road on a Saturday, arm-in-arm
> wi' your china, lookin' for fellas . . . and them lookin' for us . . .
> was as reg'lar in its way as goin' to the kirk the next morning.

It's hard to believe that the dawner along that pavement, which
went on from early in the century for thirty years, and is so universally remembered by the young of these decades, could possibly
have escaped the notice of sharp-eared-and-eyed parents.

> It would be about 1910 that we walked up and down Victoria
> Road from the Queen's Park Gate to Calder Street and back . . .
> always the same side, the east side . . . looking for clicks . . .

and the lady who was one of the strollers, when she was young
May Gilmour, adds to that . . .

> Mother would've been wild at the thought of us looking over the
> boys and sizing them up, in Victoria Road. Boy-o-boy . . .

says the ninety-year-old, with seventy years of church musi-
cianship, marriage and motherhood behind her . . .

> Boy-o-boy . . . would she had been wild!

When a single parader sits alone remembering those Saturdays she may tell of her part in it, with restraint, but when two sisters remember them together the cat is almost out of the bag.

> Mother didnae approve of the Victoria Road thing, sure she didn't?
>
> No, she did not, and if she happened along herself you'd to jink into a close till she was past.
>
> She caught me. I got into trouble for going to Victoria Road wi' Louise Parrish.
>
> Louise Parrish got into trouble without going to Victoria Road. So she did . . . twice!
>
> I was a bad girl. I used to look for clicks with Frances McGhee . . . och here I'm giving away my past. You too sister . . . wheesht!

The Cathcart Circle train service had its devotees too.

> We used to go round and round the circle, chatting up the girls on the train. In the winter that was better than Victoria Road or Great Western Road.

Sometimes a pair escaped from the town to romance in outlying villages.

> I once went out with the boy next door to Barrhead for a day out. The new buses there had red lights at the back and he told me they used red oil in Barrhead. I believed him.

A surprising part of the douce lifestyle of the first years of the century was playing Postman's Knock at parties. When Maggie Anderson's sad little romance with the soor-dook man was long past, her real courting days began.

> We werenae really introduced, we just were both playin' Postman's Knock at this friend's party and that's the way we met.

And so the serious business of walking out began.

> We used to walk round the lanes in Uddingston or maybe go for high tea at Miss Cranston's, and then get a one-and-sixpenny ticket for the King's Theatre. I liked the plays but I couldnae be doin' wi' pantomimes or music-halls. We liked the Sabbath concerts in the park fine too, right enough.

The path of that true love ran quite smoothly into marriage, but there were less happy outcomes, even among your gentry-folk that should have known better.

> I mind the works jilting. The boss's daughter was let down by this fella she was to 've married, and her brother went to have it out with him. They'd a right set-to and no matter the wrongs and right of it, the boss's son ended up arrested and put in the jail. The day he came out, all the men in his father's works downed tools and set off to carry him home on their shoulders like some big hero. My brother was one of them. Always had a great word of that chap, even though he was an Honorable.

If there had been a dour nub of pride in his father's reluctance to woo the rich Miss Brown from Hunter's Quay, there was a quieter old-world charm about Alick Murdoch's own courtship in 1919 . . . and nothing haphazard in the preparation for the setting of the proposal when it came, after months of walking his lady home after Sunday evening church.

> I did my courting around Tollcross. My young lady was Miss Katie McPhee. She was a Sabbath school teacher along with me. We kept company around things in the church and we went walking along-of the banks of the Clyde at Carmyle by the river paths there. Anyway says I to myself, 'I'm going to try to make it more definite to become allied to Katie.'
>
> So we went on a train trip together on 31 May 1919 to Aberfoyle and had our lunch at the Bailie Nicol Jarvie. Then we walked the mile to Loch Ard and hired a wee boat to row away up to the island in the middle. I took it up to the shore and we got out and sat on a nice green sward. Some of my nephews laugh at the way I say 'I plighted my troth' that day. But that's what I did . . . and Katie said 'Yes.'
>
> I mind she had a soft pink kind of flimsy scarf and on the way back down the loch a wee wind snatched it off and we watched it drifting away on the water. We didnae care but we always minded that.

And at ninety-five an old man sits back and remembers it all again.

> She was a bonnie, nice, wee girl, Katie . . . a nice wee girl.

After the First World War and through the 1920s there was a gradual relaxing of convention so that young people met, and arranged their outings without introductions to their elders. Indeed there was a new feeling that for parents to meet boy and girlfriend too soon put a serious cast on a friendship that might be no more than fleeting.

> Your parents liked to know right enough, who you were seeing and where you were going, but there was no asking permission. You'd 've laughed at that. You just met up at the kirk or the school gate or going to work on the train, and he might ask you to the pictures or for a walk wi' a poke of sweeties. When I was in love with James Henderson at about fifteen, we went walks wi' sweeties.

Sometimes parties were got up for a bit of matchmaking that took the wrong turning.

> I went to a party that was thrown to get Rob Gibson to click with Chrissie Hendry the butcher's daughter. But here it was *me* he phoned after, and Mistress Hendry never spoke to my mother again. When we were courting Rob and I, if we were too long in the close at night my big brother Henry would come out to the one-up landing, and lean over the banister shouting me up . . . too big for his boots him!

There was no great hurry in that romance.

> Six years we went steady before we got married. Went walks and dancing at the Plaza, and the pictures of course. The picture house in Sauchiehall Street was lovely. It had a palm-court and goldfish and there were cages of singing birds. It was nice going there with your boyfriend.

Over the decade they met at parties and kirks, there were chance introductions and engineered coincidences. But by the late 1920s, holidays, no longer just a whim of the toffs, opened up a whole new field of possible 'clicks'. Meeting on piers and promenades at the Glasgow Fair was generally held to be a chancy foundation for serious romance . . . but there were those which survived the holidays.

I met my Jack on the Irish boat. I was goin' my holidays wi' my sister. She was kind of flirty and she was away somewhere on the boat gettin' off wi' a bunch of campers while I was bein' sea-sick. I was just sittin' in a corner wearin' my blue hat wi' the pink rose on it, wishin' I was dead. He came over, this chap, all concerned to ask if I was all right and he took me a walk round the deck. He was in a boardin' house in Coleraine and I was across the water at Greencastle and two days later he came over in a wee boat and walked along the shore lookin' for the wee sick lassie in the blue hat. It was very romantic . . . I had a most romantic life.

Back home this romance thrived, with Sunday walks and wee cups of tea or McCallum ice-creams at Muirend. And then came the introductions to the family.

He was very early invited home was Jack. You didn't just take them in right away mind. But Jack was that respectable. He had a gold watch you see. My mother thought he was *very* nice and that I had landed lucky. It was the gold watch I think really. But I did have a very quiet genteel lad there for my intended. A real nice person.

Family involvements were not always of the kind where a dignified father eyed a young man from hair-shed to best boots to judge whether he was a fit mate for a beloved daughter. Rose Baker remembers the very different role played by her aunt Kate.

My aunt Kate was one that liked a wee refreshment, and she used to go to The Snaffles pub in Howard Street. She met a chap there she thought would just do me fine, so she took me there and introduced me. Then we all had a wee drink and went for our high tea at the Queen Anne Restaurant, and we just clicked, him and me . . . got on like a house-on-fire. I mind his first present to me was a manicuring-set. That was a laugh for I was never done bitin' my nails!

Flowers, manicure sets, sweeties, fur-backed gloves and letters were all aids to courtship over the years, and by the 1930s and '40s the telephone was a new boon to shy and very young suitors.

'I was thirteen when I first went out with a boy in about 1941,' recalls Maisie Dean of Hyndland.

It was mostly on the phone that chaps made dates and he phoned me, then after a bit of hummin' and hawing, he asked me to go to a Scout dance. I mind thinkin' my mother wouldnae let me. But she did for she ken't his mother. I wore a flowery crepey de chine dress down to below my knees. It had a Peter Pan collar too and tassels. He was about the same age's me and he walked me home and gave me a wee cheeper in the close. Then he came in and waited, all red-faced, till his father came for him, because it was nearly half past ten. I didnae tell my friends about that bit because they all did real kissing wi' real fellas. I think.

If you believe all you hear, the shy manouevres of meeting, courting and holding hands, that used to be the way of it, are dead as mutton and the whole caboodle a thing of the past. But no doubt there are still lassies who giggle and plot, and gauche lads who agonise over an opening gambit, and whether they call it 'winching' or just 'going out' find it every whit as romantic as their young grandfathers.

WEE MAN ROUND THE CORNER

There was aye a time for peever and a time for scraps and hunch-cuddy.
You never kent who di'tated that . . . the seasons just came roon.

Take marbles now. Since the 1890s marbles have been various-
ly big plunkers, steelies, brown clay dawds, white jauries; and
glassies with their mysterious twists of colour inside, sometimes
winkled out of lemonade bottles, sometimes bought in packets
by plutocrat weans. Whatever the name, stuff or size, they were
all bools, and games of marbles clicked and bounced on, and
mothers made wee bags to jingle them in, through three wars,
depression and boom. The best-remembered game of bools
was the one they called Moshie. It had interpretations enough
to merit a handbook by itself, but it was played in young days
around 1912 in Pollokshaws, with each player putting two or
three bools into a chalked ring or a dirt circle on the ground.

There was a lot of argy-bargying and counting-out for first shot at
trying to skech out as many's you could. You kep' what you skeched
out. If it was goin' too easy the boss-man used to toughen it up and
make it 'wee man round the corner' for the next game. Then you'd
to shoot your bool round past your crook't knee and ankle.

But long before these versions there was a kind of moshie in the
1850s described by Walter Freer in his memoirs.

You needed your bunnet for moshie, and a ball. You laid your bunnet against a tenement wall and you all took turns to roll the ball
into the cap from the kerb. When you got it in you'd to breenge

across the street and touch the other wall before him that's bunnet it was, took the ball out of your cap and creeshed you wi' it.

There were 101 things to do with balls of course. Many a wee lassie who played ball-beds in the 1890s lived to be great-granny to one still bouncing the ball around chalk grids in the 1960s.

> I mind yet the dunt it gave you when you touched a line and had to sit out until the next time round.
>
> And d'you mind a-leerie? You could play it on your lone. How did it go again . . . ? Oh aye . . .
>
> One, Two, Three a-leerie
> Four, Five, Six a-leerie
> Seven, Eight, Nine a-leerie
> Ten a-leerie Post-man.
>
> And you stotted your ball off of the pavement on to the wall a lot of different ways, under your leg and birling round and clapping between bounces. You just went on and on till you missed . . . oh aye I liked a-leerie.

They all liked a-leerie and they all liked jinkers and other ball, catch and chase games. But, as the present-day granny who was Betty Laurie with ringlets and big bows in the First World War years, says,

> I didn't like being het.

'Het' . . . nobody fancied being 'het', whatever the game. But if there was one thing worse than being het it was to be called 'It' instead. 'It' was if you were cissy or English (which was much the same thing) or Edinburgh, which was worse than either.

> You always had your het for hide and seek. You'd to count-out to get who was het.

But apart from counting rhymes to find the chaser, there was a wee two-liner scold for the miserable class of het who lurked around the den instead of going out fearlessly searching.

> 'You're moochin' the den
> You big fat hen'

That was a right sore insult, near as bad as when you'd cliped
on someone and got your come-uppance for that.
'Tell-tale-tit, your granny cannae knit.'

The counting-out jingles were legion and better remembered
than lots of games,

> Azeenti-Teenti-Figary Fell
> Ell Dell Dom-in-ell
> Urky Purky Taury Rope
> An Tan Toosie Joke
> You are HET

or, and this time with the line of players holding out two fists
in front to be cuffed one at a time by the boss-man doing the
counting-out,

> One potottie, Two potottie, Three potottie, Four
> Five potottie, Six potottie, Seven potottie, More!

and at More! the last fist to be hit was put behind the back and
the whole rigmarole went on again . . . and again. Last fist left
was 'het'.

> It took that long sometimes that you got shouted in before you
> were done wi' the pototties, and that was the ball on the slates for
> your tig or whatever.

Azeentie Teentie was dying by the 1940s, but the fists were
still potottied and the new Tic-Tac sorting out first shots at
things. Tossing a penny lacked the ritual of any of them, and
anyway the penny had usually disappeared into Ogo-Pogo eyes
or chocolate chewing-nuts before the game was planned.

Then there was jumping-ropes! Skipping is remembered
with joy across all the years from the 1880s to times present. A
solitary wean could just wind her rope round her hands to shorten
it and get on with the job alone, but it was the eruption of small
girls in a fankle of ropes into the playground when the bell clanged
. . . and the cry going up 'No ender', that most remember.

You done your jumpin'-ropes in the street or the playground or maybe the back green. I was a rare wee skipper . . . that would be about 1899 . . . two an' out was two jumps in a cawin' rope and out the other side . . . And d'you mind of 'keep the pot boilin'? That was when the next lassie didnae wait on you finishing, but came in the same caw you went out.

Through the 1920s and '30s they skipped, backwards and forwards, arms crossed, two turns to a jump, two jumps to a turn, red-faced, breathless, and gasping out their rhyming chants like metronomes.

> Matthew, Mark, Luke, John
> Ask the Ro-mans where they're gaun
> If they say they're gaun to Rome
> Hit them wi' a tattie scone.

And in a Glasgow always beset by 'feeling' between Billys and Dans there had to be a counterblast.

> Matthew, Mark, Luke, John
> Ask the Proddies where they're gaun
> If they say they're gaun to kirk
> Whack them wi' a great big stick.

Those who neither knew, nor cared, a bawbee about Romans or Proddies had other immortal 'poentry' for their skips,

> A hunner and ninety-nine
> My faither fell in a byne
> My mither came oot wi' the washin' cloot
> And skelped his big behind.

That was in the 1930s. By the '50s they had . . .

> High, low, slow, mejum,
> Dolly-rocky, pepper, wishy.

The first four were just what you'd think, dolly-rocky was jumpin' side to side, pepper was quick, and wishy your own special trick. You shouted to the enders what you were going to do and they did the rope right for that.

Indeed the skinny-ma-linky wee lassie of any decade that could twinkle her feet like magic in the ropes was more of a queen to the others than the one that could rattle off her tables or get ten out of ten for her spellings, or even the one who could sit on her hair. The lady who was skipping as wee Maggie Anderson in 1896 puts it . . .

> You were no use if you couldnae skip or peever.

Ah peevers! Peevers were edged from chalk-bed to chalk-bed by the toe, as the player hoppetied her way along in the correct order without the peever coming to rest on a line. It was played in the gaiters and button boots of the turn of the century, the bar-and-button shoes of the teen years and the canvas sannies of the 1920s.

> And *we* played it in the 1940s

protests one of the four elegant and accomplished Gibson sisters who were hopscotching throughout these ten years, in Croftfoot.

> We had *beautiful* peevers, with our initials on them . . . personalised! We played outside, but we played on the blue-square-patterned carpet in the living room as well. Just the thing that carpet!

Some remember singing-games as street-play. But they were the children of the very early years. After that singing-games belonged to indoor parties or the Brownies. For Mrs Margaret Henderson they were out-of-door games and she can still sing clear and softly the songs she shouted as a lusty five-year-old:

> In and out the windows,
> In and out the windows,
> In and out the windows,
> As you have done before.

And her old hands did the dance that once her feet had done as a follow-my-leader ring game long ago, when Uddingston was countryside, outside the city.

Around 1910 young girls like Cathie Anderson were still singing in the open air and gathering flowers as they went.

I mind, clear as clear, the smell of wild garlic when we used to go up round Cathcart Castle yonder, every May Day, to gather celandines. And we sang going up that hill . . .

> You must wake and call me early,
> Call me early Mother dear,
> For I'm to be queen of the May, Mother
> I'm to be queen of the May.

Summer days were always long and to be filled by more than singing-games and skipping. There were the young adaptations of adult sports, played with whatever make-do implements lay at hand. Mr William Stevenson remembers playing golf.

> Aye, we played at golf on the field behind Harriet Street. You dug a wee hole first. Then you bent a bit wire off a fence into a kind of club shape. After that you collected yon washer-rings off of ginger bottles and put them on for the handle. You were a'ready then to hit a bit cork to the hole from so far away. Sometimes you could do it in two shots or three. Other times it took about a dozen. You didnae have toys or that bought to you. You just invented them.

But he's gone over to the Establishment since those days.

> I've been a member of Cowglen Golf Club and Barassie, these past thirty or so years,

and it's 'bowls' at an expensive club now where once it was moshie in a dirt ring. He considers . . .

> but I'm no' sure I enjoy all that better than yonder at Harriet Street wi' the bit fencin' and the ginger-washers.

There were other rule-books games for other boys to copy.

> 'Where are you goin' Alick?' . . . Mother out the kitchen window.
>   'Goin' to the cricket Mother,' . . . me wi' my best bat all ready to play in the farmer's field.
>   'You see that stretch of garden you were to weed last week Alick?'
>   'Aye Mother.'
>   'There'll be no cricket the day till you've all that done.'

I knew there would be no cricket that afternoon . . . I think the iron entered my soul that day and I've never been that keen on gardening ever since.

Footb'll and cricket were the main things we played at in Tollcross ninety year ago. That's where you got your discipline

or maybe just from the lady at the kitchen window.

Even some girls endured the discipline of football. Nellie Edgar played around 1919.

You all played. You ca'ed it seven-a-side, no matter you'd six to play or twenty-five . . . seven-a-side it was, I always bagsed to be the goalie because I didnae like it rough. The goalie was in the game right enough but no' in the stramash.

Sometimes the goal posts in street football were stones or jackets, or just chalk marks on walls and then, as in street cricket, only a puff of chalk dust was evidence that a goal had been missed or a wicket taken.

But it's a panting, peching business, all that skipping, stotting, tigging and footb'll, and there's another chapter ahead for more playing. Meantime tomorrow is the Sabbath and that day and its rituals leave memories that are just as indelible in their way as moshie or jinkers.

11

SLOTTED INTO PEWS

You'd think to hear some folk now that in the old days it was 'No, no, no!' that you didnae do this and you didnae do that on the Sabbath . . . that you just went about all douce and glunchy. Well right enough you didnae play in the street or do dice and card games in the house. But Sunday was for a lot of things you did do . . . things that made it different from other days.

So it was. It was for kirk and Sabbath school, for Sunday dinners and walks and visiting. And fortifying the tribe for the rigours of the day was the cooked breakfast.

It was porridge through the week but, oh aye, we always started Sundays wi' a cooked breakfast. That was one of the highlights of the week, the eight of us sitting there at our cooked breakfasts. Mother couldnae have done it very easy on a labourin' man's wage, but we'd always our sausage or maybe very occasionally a wee bit scrambled egg, on a Sunday.

Breakfast down and the dishes washed, the next item on the Sunday agenda was the walk to the kirk. For some it was close to home.

We were just marched a wee bit along the street to our kirk for it was part of the same block as our tenement.

For others, like young Joe and Willie Kyle around 1910, there was a fair old hike.

We walked the three miles to the kirk on a Sunday morning, then home for dinner and back again to the Sunday school in the afternoon. There were kirks nearer home mind you, but that was the one where my father was and where we were baptised.

For yet others the walk to the church was a modest flaunting of
the Sunday braws.

> My friend's family and mine always walked together to church, with
> the children in front so we didn't get up to mischief. That would
> be about 1912. Margaret and I usually craiked at our mothers to
> get us clothes the same. I remember one summer we'd coats alike,
> but for colour . . . mine was gold satin with a hat to match, and she
> was the exact same but blue. Oh very dressy we were on Sundays! It
> wouldn't've done to get the satin coats splashed with rain so if it
> was wet we took the white tram.

Having reached their various kirks, well-nigh the whole citizenry
of Glasgow was slotted into pews for the next hour or more . . .
sometimes much more.

> We'd get there and in we used to troop to our pew. There was
> Bill, the eldest, first; then me, then Elizabeth, then Jim and Meg
> and George, and then Mother and Faither.
>
> I mind when Bill got away to the far end he used to sit down
> and hunch up his shoulders, turning towards the wall a wee bit. He
> was s'posed to be kind of pious and he used to take down the sermon
> in shorthand so's he could give the gist to the Sunday school in the
> afternoon. Anyway he always looked like he was taking down the whole
> service, but I knew fine he was readin' his Dixon Hawke till the time of
> the preachin' came on. Then he *had* to listen to get his notes right.

Other children spent a fair bit of the service puzzling over
strange statements in hymns and psalms about 'throwing weary
pilgrimages' and suchlike.

> When I was just wee I couldnae understand why a green hill should've
> had a city wall, so what did it matter that it was without one. The hymn
> I liked best was 'The Lord's my Shepherd' . . . but again in it there was
> that head that I thought was messy with all the 'oil and oint' on it . . .
> Every time I sing them even now in the kirk, at eighty-eight, the same
> ideas I had then, come to mind. And there's me standing there, old and
> crabby-lookin' and inside I'm smilin' away and just wee again.

Sometimes, of course, there was a baptism. Families were big
and all but the youngest (the poke-shakin's) were well-acquainted
with christenings.

> I mind when you went to the kirk wi' a christenin' party and then
> came out after, your mother or your pa had a wee piece or a bit
> cake wi' them and the thing to do was, that if your wean was a
> lassie you gie'd the chuck to the first man you met and if your
> wean was a boy, you gie'd it to the first woman.

That was your own kirk, but occasionally there was a visit to a
service in another church, perhaps a parent's childhood congregation. Young Anne Gardner went sometimes as a treat, taking
the red tram out Cathedral Street.

> I used to go sometimes with my father to the Barony Church. He
> used to be Barony when he was a young man at the turn of the
> century. Anyway it was a long tram ride away and there weren't
> too many trams ran on Sundays, so after church, while we were
> waiting for a 'car' home, we used to go into the Tallie's shop for
> a McCallum. Mother would've been horrified . . . but I don't
> suppose we rushed home to tell her.

That tram ride was their lull before Sunday dinner but other
fathers took the weans for walks to whet their appetites. Father
Fotheringham took his brood to the flagpole at Bellahouston
Park after the kirk, or to the Maxwell Park. The Guthrie
crocodile was led by their father round Victoria Park and the
Fossil Grove. The Edgars went to Pollok.

> Sometimes between kirks, morning and afternoon, Father took us
> to the Policies, or out the Cowglen for a walk, and I mind some-
> times of seeing Sir John Stirling-Maxwell out walking or driving.
> He would be coming home from kirk too, for he sat under the
> minister at Eastwood up the hill. Mother didnae go on the walks.
> She was at home makin' dinner.

These were the stepping-out walks for those who lived on the
outskirts of the city. But there were other less energetic after-
church strolls nearer to the upmarket heartlands of the city, and
Great Western Road and the crescents of the west end were
thronged at noon on Sundays with families making their leisurely
way home from morning service. Some socialised with each

other in chatting groups, some made stately progress along the pavement, the ladies nodding under the bonnets of the 1890s, the cabbage-rose cart-wheels of Edwardian summers, and the 1920s' cloches. Their menfolk lifted hats (from lum to bowler in their fashion) and swaggered, ever so slightly, their silver-knobbed walking canes and rou'ed up gamps.

Survivors of that Sunday parade admit that there was a showing-off of well-put-on families in their Sunday bests, but point out piously too that they would no more have gone into God's house in unseemly claddings than they would have insulted a hostess so, in her home.

Then it was back to Sunday dinner. The family home from its walk, hungry and expectant, Mother emerged with ashet and tureen, Father said grace, and they were off!

> My mother wouldn't have thought Sunday was Sunday without a joint of meat . . . beef or a gigot of lamb with roast potatoes. Soup first usually, and then the likes of a steam pudding or a jam rolly.

Across the city it was the same ritual but a different menu.

> Roast beef . . . never! Roast beef was just in stories. But my ma made a rare meat-loaf and we'd that wi' champit tatties that had onions through them, and for afters, a suet puddin' in a big bowl. My pa was reared up in the country and he said what he called his bethankit when we were done eatin'. That was Sunday dinner.

Except during a few weeks in the summer there was afternoon Sunday school. Two old ladies drink their tea at a winter fire and forget their angina and rheumatics in quiet laughter over remembered lessons.

> I loved the Sunday school Dorothy, did you? D'you mind learning the Bible stories and getting yon wee tickets from the teacher with golden texts and pictures on them?
>
> Yes, and rhyming off the books of the Bible and the Beatitudes and bits of the Psalms.
>
> Right enough yes . . . and the Catechism. I hated the Catechism.

We sat there and giggled or poked each other. But we must've listened to something, sure we must?

Ah but I didn't always know what the texts an' that meant, and definitely *not* the Catechism. But now it's funny, they come easy to me and I think maybe I know what they mean after carrying them in my head all these years.

Not everyone was so keen.

I didnae like it much. I just tholed it because I was sent. I was the age for Sunday school before the First World War and I don't mind that I learned much. I would be well enough behaved but I never took up with the kirk when I'd just myself to please.

On the other hand Jack Bute's camsteerie ongoings and verdicts on the Kirk Session, when his Sunday school class observed the Communion service from the gallery, didn't have a lasting blight on his commitment since he has been a devoted elder and session clerk himself for many a long year.

We used to lean over and pass cheeky whispers along the pew about the elders as they filed in, all like black and white penguins. We used to bring feathers to drop over, then we watched them floatin' down to settle on some lady's best hat or a man's good suit.

Another less-than-righteous lad remembers offering more than the coin of the realm to the collection.

The superintendent used to tell us at the end of the Sunday school how much the offering was, and where it would go, and I always remember him standing up there looking all stern, without a smile on his face. 'Today's collection came to 13s 6p, a nice black button and an Irish ha'penny . . . and it goes to the Tent Hall Mission and the Leprosy Society.'

Then June came and the flower service, when they all brought lupins and fruit for the sick, and got their prizes for good attendance or high marks in the Bible exam. After that it was the summer holidays. That didn't mean out to play, of course, but the start of the really long walks that were a feature of Glasgow Sabbaths, until car runs and sprawling at the television flabbied walking muscles.

On these summer Sundays the Fotheringham treks went far beyond Bellahouston flag-pole.

> Sometimes we walked from Dumbreck to Queen's Park and took a tram to Eastwood Toll. This was before the First World War. Then we walked the four miles to Newton Mearns village. There was a nice tearoom there . . . just a house really with a verandah and pillars. I can still taste the scones we got there, but the thing I liked the best was the wee pot of jam you got to yourself. After that if it was a nice day you walked all the way home, maybe eight or nine miles, down by Spiersbridge and through the Pollok estate.

Others walked to Eaglesham or Cathkin Braes . . . or northwards to Chapelton Loch or out over the Switchback to Milngavie, and the only refuelling for the long walk home was often a cup of tea or an ice-cream cone — and if your pa was strict about the Sabbath, maybe neither.

Next on the day's timetable, to nail the lie that old-time Sundays were long deserts of boredom and inactivity, was the visiting . . . from or to the clans of aunties and uncles most folk had before families shrank to two-point-five. It was always for high tea.

> Goin' was much better'n havin' them, for you could eat what you liked and there was no F.H.B. (d'you mind being told 'family hold back'?).

If there was evening church, friends often came back after the service. Young Maggie Anderson loved that, ninety years ago, and enjoys resurrecting the old scene now.

> Father used to bring home Dr Smith and Mr Turnbull the organist, after the kirk, and we all sang hymns and sacred songs round the piano with the candles lit on the sconces. We all got to choose our favourites and folk used to stop on the street outside to listen. My, that was lovely on a Sunday night. Then we went to bed and the grown-ups had their suppers.

Mrs Nancy Watt, though, squirms at memories of the tail-end to similar Sunday evenings in her home a few years later.

All the young folk came to our house after church to sing round the piano with my sister playing hymns and suitable Sunday songs . . . that was nice. But here my grandpa stayed with us and at ten o'clock sharp he used to come in and tell them it was time to go home.

Even that wasn't so bad, but then he used to stand at the door and, as they went out, he shook hands with each one and said, 'Joy be with you . . . joy be with you.' He was an old saint really, but I was so embarrassed.

That then was the shape and programme of the Sabbath itself from breakfast to evening blessing. It was regular, planned, obligatory. The almost universal practice of church-going from Victorian times throughout the first third of this century suggests a bland obedience to sameness in religious matters which was far from the truth. They all went to kirk certainly but, in over forty conversations, eleven or more denominations were claimed, from Wee Free to Roman Catholic.

My father was Wee Free, so he didn't hold with Christmas.
I was converted to the Brethren when I was a girl.
We went to the Methody in Cathcart.

A lot of Highland folk like myself took to the Congregationals . . .

We were Episcopals, when I was a girl in the 1890s and after. I think that was because my folks had been estate workers and they all attended the estate chapel. Anyway, when I got wed I went wi' my man to the Presbyterian kirk, but after the Piskies it was a wee bit dull no' to take your part in the service. So sometimes at Easter, just to mind me of old times, I used to slip away to the Anglican Church at Polmadie.

The youthful Marie Condie out at Uddingston didn't sit like Buddha waiting for enlightenment to strike her in her own kirk, she went out seeking for it.

When I got to be about fourteen I used to go to the Hallelujah Hall to see if I could get converted. I wasnae really sure what that meant . . . but I knew when it happened right enough. It was good there. We sang songs and choruses, sometimes solo, sometimes all joinin' together, rousin' and loud. Then cups of tea came round.

Another who went out after more nourishment at night, when duty had been rendered at her own church and Sunday school, was May Gilmour, just after the turn of the century.

> When we were about fourteen or fifteen my friend and I used to take a ha'penny one in the tram to go to the congregational church near St Andrew's Halls to hear Ambrose Shepherd preaching. He was gettin' on by then but oh my, could he preach? The place was packed every time and people sat on the pulpit steps and stood all round the back. I used to grit my teeth all the way home in the tramcar . . . 'I'll be good, oh I'll be good!'

Eighty-year-old memories of gritted teeth and vows of righteousness are surely a fair tribute to powerful preaching.

Scots have never easily knuckled under to the heresies of those who disagreed with them. Most especially not in matters of religion. Having seen the light, offered it to their brethren and been rejected, rather than sit on, quibbling and chawnering, they have preferred to take their truth with them and set up new denominations round the corner.

> Our wee Original Secession kirk was quite bien, because a lot of the first elders in it, had been kind of thinkin' folk that had come out the ordinary kirk over their beliefs. It was a well-run wee place wi' a decent building and a paid minister . . . and it didnae be that on the six pennies Willie and me, an' Bessie and Maggie an' James an' George put in the plate, or even Mother and Faither's wee thrupennies, there were lawyers and doctors an' teachers wi' a wee bit more behind them to help things along.
>
> That was the Original Seceders,* the Auld Lichts, then another wee breakaway of folk that thought they were an improvement were called the New Lichts. Later they came together again, the Auld and the New, to make the United Presbyterians.

---

* The reasons for the breakaway in the eighteenth century of certain churchmen from the old Kirk were complex . . . a skirlie of objections to the placing of ministers by the laird's patronage and also an alarmed conviction that the idea of reasoned interpretation of Scripture was a do-it-yourself blasphemy, fudging belief in 'saving' by God's grace alone.

But however marked the differences were among these, they were all splinters of the Reformed Church. The truly great Glasgow divide has always been the Grand Canyon between Protestant and Catholic. For over 300 years Proddy folk of whatever caste have been making their way along one street to their building while their Catholic neighbours have made theirs to chapel on the next street. Not many like Lily Timlin had the ecumenical experience of being both.

> My mother lost her man in the First World War and after a while she married again, so we went away to live wi' my stepfather and I didnae see anything of my own father's lot for a long while. My stepfather was very strict and I was at the kirk and Sunday school every week. There was no playin' or workin' on Sundays and I mind that if a button came off of your shoe, like, you didnae get to sew it on so you couldnae even go a walk. Anyway, then my mother died and when I was about fourteen I came back to live wi' my own father's ma. I mind the day I arrived alone at her house, and sittin' there talkin' to this granny that I hardly knew. There was me eyein' up all the holy pictures in the room and just wonderin' to myself . . . then when we were at our tea my granny came away wi' her bombshell.
>
> 'You ken Lily, that you're a Catholic?' says she.
>
> 'You're kiddin'!' says I, for if there was one thing I knew I wisnae . . . it was a Catholic. After all these years in the Sunday school! I couldnae be. So I told her. Well she didnae say any more then, but on the Sunday she took me to St Mary's and after the service, sure enough, the priest brought out the Baptism register and there was me, 'Lily Timlin, born 31 January 1914 baptised 4 February by the Reverend Father Reilly.' Well, murder-polis, whit a thing! It was like I was two people. Then to make up for the wicked years at the Sunday school I went for about six weeks' instruction at the Helpers of the Holy Soul. I took a great notion there to Mother Agatha. She was nice. She talked to me and took me to sales of work and fêtes and suchlike. So you see I've aye been a bit of both really . . . never felt sore about the one or the other.

And that's maybe a sensible place to leave the Sunday doings of the good citizens of Glasgow, reconciled in the two people who were Lily Timlin.

12

TAM TUNNOCK DID THE PURVEY

I can trace our family back ten generations and I found out a funny thing about that. I had over 500 great-great-great-great-great-great-great-great grandparents. Fancy that! But there was really only two I knew about, out of all of them. They were up before the Kirk Session and made to get married. So weddings have been goin' a long time in our family. That one was in 1602.

Others too can pin down two or more of the Army of ancestors whose lines finally converged on Glasgow to produce them. Mrs Margaret Kent has a tangible little item to bring an old family romance to life.

My grannie gave me a ring that was given to my great-great-great grandmother at her betrothal in 1703.

It lies gleaming on her hand as bright and fresh as the day it was slipped on to Bethia Hall's finger when Queen Anne was on the throne. The date 1703 is engraved inside and, beside it, the initials BH. Neither shank nor setting is crudely cut as in many old rings, but expertly worked and set with amethyst and garnet. With the ring has come down just enough of the family's history to tantalise and intrigue.

Bethia's father Nicholas Deschamp was a Huguenot refugee who came from France in the 1690s, started to collect rags round the doors and then set up his own small paper-making place near the Snuff Mill bridge at Cathcart. There, it's said, he made the paper for the Darien Scheme documents . . . and presumably

93

enough money to dower Bethia well enough to match her fine ring.

The earliest mention of celebrations after a marriage ceremony is from the mid-1800s and is therefore once-removed from direct memory. Mrs Janet Purvis of Eastwoodhill House describes the occasion as it was told to her. The bride and groom seem to have been young Victorian moderns, well ahead of their time by being wed in church after the English custom, rare in Glasgow.

> After the service they went to Hughes' and Pinkertons', a high-class restaurant at Bridgeton Cross, for the reception. My aunt was the bridesmaid and so she met the best man that day, on leave from India, and they got married on his next leave.

Then there was a gentry wedding in the 1890s, of a much-loved local laird who displayed a hapless choice of words to present his bride to the local tenantry.

> My mother was brought up on the laird's estate. Her father, you see, was a labourer to Sir George. Mother could talk about the tenantry balls and suchlike that she got to, but she liked best to remember the day Sir George got wed. She just loved the laird, did my mother. Anyway when he brought his bride home, a year or so before the turn of the century, the estate carters met the newly weds at the old station. They loused the horses from their yokes, went into the shafts them-selves and pulled the carriage home to the Big House. At the entrance the laird called for all the workers to toast his new wife. 'This is my lady' he says 'and she's better than she's bonnie.' I suppose he meant *even* better, but though she was nice, right enough, she was an unbraw woman so she was. So the men were never quite sure.

Maybe Sir George was a wee frog in a big puddle compared to his future king, but the laird's reputation was above the kind of reproach that that popular but roving monarch had to put up with. But Edward had apparently sterner marriage principles for those who served him than for himself.

> I once worked under a duke and ladyship when I was about seventeen in wartime when their home was a military hospital. The duke had

been a gentleman-in-waiting to Edward VII but because there had been a divorce before their marriage he was dismissed his place at court. I thought that was kind of funny of Edward VII, sure it was?

There were great lairds like that in Scotland who owned large properties and there were wee lairds who owned small properties. But there was another category too, who were lairds of no more than their own hearthsides.

I can mind of a friend of my mother's that came from one of Glasgow's old boroughs. I used to visit her room-and-kitchen house sometimes and I heard her call her man, not Jamie that was his right name, but 'laird'. 'Put the kettle on the hob for the lassie's tea, laird' she used to say, and he answered her, 'Aye, right y'are then Mistress.'

Plain work-folk they may have been to the gaffers in Lum Hat Street but they were laird and mistress to each other. And a related quirk of Scottish life is brought out by other reminiscences and stabs of memory. More perhaps then elsewhere, women have retained a kind of par-status with their menfolk in the use of their maiden names, in conversation, in newspaper reports and in documents. Even in the end on their gravestones. There a woman may have been that bleak-sounding left-over, somebody's 'relict', but at least she's been a relict with her own name.

Laird and mistress then, in their two rooms, James Macewan and Jessie Storr, and none prouder. The tea was duly masked and served in the wedding-present china of many years before.

Other wedding treasures have survived in the rememberers' homes to be used with pride and footnote still, even among the present day's suffocating amount of gear.

See that teaspoon you're stirring your tea with, well that set came to my mother over eighty years ago as a wedding present from her bachelor brother in New Zealand. They always minded her of him. He was a doctor away in the outback and went on his rounds with his horse, and with the district nurse riding back-saddle behind him.

And there was maybe a tradition of pleasure in good cutlery, for when May Reid herself was married she added to her mother's solid silver teaspoons a present from another noteworthy source.

> I was in charge of buying gowns in Fraser's in the 1920s when young Hugh came in to learn the ropes, so I knew him pretty well when he was a laddie. By the time I was getting married he was a man though, and he took me to his family's jewellers above the Grosvenor and bought us a lovely canteen of cutlery. Nice he was, Hugh Fraser.

Money may have been tight and food short in the throes of the First World War but 'there was none of your silly wee savouries' at Maggie Anderson's wedding in 1916.

> We'd our reception in the Public Hall and Tam Tunnock did the purvey (him from the baker's shop), steak pie and potatoes and all that, and a wedding cake. It was the war mind, so there wasnae sugar for icing, just a cardboard cover all decorated wi' plaster. It looked the same's icing and the same cover went over all Tam's wedding cakes, that wartime. It was quite nice and the cake under it was lovely. We just drank juice . . . no wine or that carry-on. Couldnae afford that nonsense anyway.

Just as clear in the 95-year-old's memory were her wedding clothes.

> My rig-out was yon shot-silk taffeta in all different shadings, and I had a bokay of flowers off a friend that was a gardener at a big house. And I mind having a Leghorn straw hat wi' big-big roses round it. My man's knees were gey wobbly that day, for the wedding was in the Episcopal church and *he* was Kirk . . . didnae know all the wee ways at our service.

There must have been many a catch to the heart and in the 'I do's' of wartime marriages.

> I was married on Sandy's leave in 1917 and we'd a nice weekend at Largs for our honeymoon. Then he went away back to France . . . Just his watch came back and two-three letters. I suppose it was a bit of the Somme fighting. I never right knew where. I was that numb sittin' there wi' the telegram in my hand in the nice room and kitchen I was gettin' ready for him.

Others had happier reunions. Mrs Milree . . .

I was married six months before the Armistice and then my husband went back to France. He spoke several languages so he was a liaison officer with the Seaforths there. I was one of the lucky ones that he came back. Anyway I wore navy-blue taffeta at my wedding. It was in the parlour and it was Dr Cooper of Strathbungo married us. My father was a kirk elder there.

Through many generations it's been the marriage right of Scottish brides, rich or poor, to take up house well-tochered with presents from neighbours, friends and kin. And few new houses are short of linen, kitchenware, crockery, or little bits of silver for 'best'. But among the recollections are those of one girl whose hanselling was very sparse.

I'd no family behind me by the time I was fourteen and into service out Great Western Road. In a few years I was walkin' out wi' this chap on my afternoons off, when my mistress died. My chap Joe was on his own too, so we just got wed quiet. The only present I had, bar a new coat from him, was a tea-set that the mistress's niece gie'd me out the house. Many's the time I had washed them cups after an afternoon tea, and now here they were mine's. They were my proudest possession they dishes, for many a long year. Forbye them, we started off wi' just a few pokeshakin's he had of his mother's, a bit cutlery, a few towels a pot an' that . . . and a stick or two furniture we picked up at a sale.

A mixed marriage in Glasgow has traditionally meant the coupling of Catholic and Protestant and many a family has been thrown into confusion at the prospect. But there are, and were, other graftings and other ways of handling such matters.

I was a member of the Brethren when I married Mr Purvis and my father was very firm and wise.

'There must be no divided house. You'll go to the Glasgow Cathedral with your husband and be in the kirk there.'

That was in 1920 when Dr MacAdam Muir was minister, and I've been a member there ever since.

Most of the menfolk recall their courting days but not many can describe their own wedding attire or their bride's.

Mine's was tight at the collar but other than that I couldnae say. Jenny was in pink, was it? Or maybe pale blue. She was aye nice in blue. I mind my honeymoon better . . . just a day or two at Saltcoats. It was that cold we'd to wear jerseys in bed. No' very romantic? Oh aye, bar that, it was quite romantic.

By the early 1920s weddings were beginning to come out of parlours and into hotels; and other fashion changes were on the way among post-war brides.

I had my hair cut for the first time, the day of my wedding. It had aye been long, down to my waist then 'up' from I was eighteen. I was early to have short hair and my very first silk stockings were for my honeymoon.

Mrs Helen Stewart remembers her wedding day in 1930. By then the day of the hotel wedding was in full swing for both ceremony and reception. Church marriages too were coming in, for some to highlight the earnestness of their vows, for some as a braw setting for the great day, for others a thoroughly human mixture of both.

But *we* werenae married in church nor yet at a hotel. Nobody got wed in the Secession church (that was the Auld Lichts kirk mind). So it was our parlour at the Wellmeadow.

And she recalls the day of her nuptials with pride, pleasure and unsentimental good humour. The wedding season, of course, began the day before.

Aye, aye, the day before when I left work at the mill (you didnae go back once you were married) . . . anyway, there was a right carry-on. I was very sedate myself and I didnae think they would do these things to me. But they did. They decked me out with old lace curtains and I had to carry a chantie along the street from the mill to home. I was that mortified! It wasnae that kind at all, but they did it to me. Aye, did they no' just.

Next day the minister came in his lum hat to perform the cere-mony in the fine front room with the congoleum floor. Now

Nellie and her chap are man and wife and it's reception time. Her mother had the afters organised weeks before.

> 'It'll no' be big Nellie, but we'll do the whole thing right and have a nice Co-operative purvey.' And so we did. We'd steak pie and potatoes and peas.

And her rig-out for the day?

> I wore a blue dress at 19s. 11d. out of the C&A . . . stiff taffeta. I got a real nice coat too. The first really good thing I ever had. And I had a straw hat forbye.
>
> We called that my going-away coat, but here we werenae goin' anywhere. We didnae have a honeymoon but I had a right good setting-down in a two-rooms-and-kitchen with all the wedding-presents. Nice presents . . . cream jugs and wee biscuit plates and suchlike. The biggest was from a brother-in-law in the London Police. He sent a Sheffield carving set. I just looked at it and laughed.
>
> 'What do I do wi' that?' says I, for it was mostly mince we had. Anyway it was my man's pride and joy that carving set.

A wedding at the same period of the early 1930s *was* in the church, the fine Trinity (now Glencairn) in Pollokshields. Photographs show a beautiful bride in a simple white gown surrounded by black and white morning dress and bonnie chapleted bridesmaids in dresses that were slender and close-fitting from shoulder to knee, then flaring out in frothing lace and lover's knots. The lady guests in the arch of the doorway are in ankle-length coats with huge fur collars and snug cloche hats. No Co-op purvey at that reception in Gordon Street's Grosvenor Function Suite, but a fitting menu to follow an elegant Glasgow wedding of between the wars.

Where there was no mother there were hazards to arranging a wedding, especially two years into the Second World War with all its regulations and restrictions.

> When Jimmy and I were to get married, we'd each to get our papers for the Registry. He got his when he was off and I got mine's

when I was off. I was on the buses y'see . . . shifts. Well all the purvey was laid out at my granny's and him and me were to meet our witnesses at the Registry. My papers were for the Registry right enough, but I suppose *he* thought you went on somewhere else for the actual ceremony, because the papers he had were for a church. So they wouldnae do us at the Registry. Oh my, what a carry-on! An' the purvey all ready at my granny's! Anyway they phoned a minister and we just went round to his manse and got married there.

So, high-spired church with Lohengrin, or scramble in the Registry with purvey at Granny's, each was the climax to the winching and the catch, the hopeful prelude to happy married life.

But not everyone found bliss in marriage delivered as promised, and some indeed wondered if it had all been worthwhile. Polly Strang tells of her teaching days in the 1940s.

I remember a Mrs Ritchie comin' up to the school to have it out that her girl was being unfairly got at. The family had all been right wee handfuls for the staff and soon the mother and this teacher were having a confidential chat about her difficult man and her hullarackit children. She was ready to go away quite calmed down, and then she turned back . . . 'Mind I sometimes think yous old maids has the best of it . . . after yous gets over the affront of not bein' asked.'

Should we let her have the last word on marriage? Why not? She was a realistic wee woman and she must have come to terms with Mr Ritchie, or else herself been 'got at' because before Polly Strang's teaching time was out at that school there were several more infant Ritchies either in the school or at various stages on the way.

13

THREE MILES WAS NOTHING WI' YOUR GIRD

So, Sundays over, the week's work and play began again and there's another batch of outdoor playing fads and fancies to be prised out of elderly memory banks. When winter's football, skating and ice-slides were past, when finger and ear chaps were healed and the Snowfire ointment away at the back of the bathroom press, then all the joys of the long warmer days came and they took up again the round of things they had done last summer.

That was when the call of the yonder came to bairns, from single-ends to Jordanhill mansions, and wheels . . . any kind of wheels were the thing.

> We made bogies. You got a plank and a pair of old pram wheels, wi' a swivel bar and a bit of clo'es line for steering. We lived up Rotten Row way and we used to start wi' the bogie up the top of John Street and go breengin' down across George Street. It was a miracle we didnae crash a van or a cart. We never killed nobody either.

They were no more effete in fancier suburbs and the boy that was Ian Fotheringham of the 1912–13 band of bogie-ists was, if not guilty of manslaughter, at least skeely with the swivel-bar, and lucky at that.

> We used to go pelting down the slope into Pollokshields station and out the other side. Once when I was doing that I went right into the crowd disgorging from my father's train, and here I scattered all these City gents in their bowlers. There they were all scuttling clear of my bogie. I suppose it was funny but I got the worst skelping I ever had in my life.

Some girls too tucked up their petticoats and let their hair stream out behind them as they hurtled down the hills on the boys' bogies. But an indulgent brother might make a more 'suitable' vehicle for a quiet sister.

> I had a beautiful china-headed doll called Daisy and the boys made me a sort of barrow box-on-wheels. We called that the Daisy Express.

That wee sister was not a tomboy, but maybe Daisy was. For she, and her companion doll Ida, had a real doll's pram forbye the cart. But tomboy or no she was part of a two-pram two-doll family in bien Nithsdale Road.

There were bicycles, too, over all the eras remembered, in various forms from bone-shaker to Raleigh magnificence, but those who didn't actually have bikes or bogies were philosophical. Who wanted a bike anyway? Bikes were posh and cissy. Wheels, whatever the form, were transport.

> Nobody round us had bikes and weans didnae have prams for to get bogie wheels (it was just shawls they got taken out in). But we did have girds and cleeks and we thought they took us just as fast. You would girn at a half-mile walk to go a message for your ma, but three miles planned-out wi' your gird was nothing . . . maybe five times round the public library or two or three blocks of Alexandra Parade . . . that was nothin' wi' your gir' and cleek. The flat iron yins ran quite sweet, but the lassies had mostly wooden ones that bounced and wobbled . . . nae use! But well, a lassie couldnae expect . . .

What a lassie couldnae expect was mercifully left unsaid, and we passed thirty-five years on, to the 1940s. The last recollection of real hoop running was from those war years, but girds were going out by then, and the cleeker of that memory found few to travel with. Her hoop mouldered for twenty years in a cellar until she passed it on to children with shiny pedal-cars who didn't know what to do with it.

> D'you mind biff-bats? Wee rubber balls on an elastic pinned to a bat like a ping-pong bat, and you kep' up twenty or thirty hits, or

> maybe fifty if you were good at it. But they were 'hi-li' bats when they came back in the 1950s,

says one of the delightful and humorous ladies (of the person-alised peevers) and, as if conducted by Sir Hugh Roberton, their precision so immaculate, three of them standing in the gleaming kitchen of the youngest burst out chanting, and with actions (hi-li-ing across three throats) . . .

> Mary Queen of Scots had her head chopped off
> Her head chopped off, her head chopped off
> Mary Queen of Scots had her head chopped off
> HEAD!   CHOPPED!   OFF!

Girds, tigs and hets and high-low water . . . organised, strict-ruled and innocent . . . ah innocent! Even city-core weans were innocent in the days before the 1950s . . . sure they were?

> Box-beds, bogies and statues. I played the whole jing-bang in the 1920s. But playing in the street was more interesting. Quite a lot of nasty wee tricks we played there . . . like chap doors and run.

Mrs Helen Stewart, as lively now in her kirk care flat as she was years ago in the school shed two miles away, remembers plan-ning the nasty wee tricks that sent the giggles echoing down the closes of her childhood. Ah yes, for all their being mim and respectful to their elders (virtues much claimed by those who were the children of long ago) they played a mischief or two that would bring howls of 'hooligan' from them now, about similar delinquents of today.

Some swopped around the doormats outside various tene-ment homes, and that door-chapping was a simple version of the long-time favourite of bell-ringing. Glasgow doorbells have been mischievously pushed, pulled and jangled for certainly over 100 years.

> I think I pulled every bell in Stevenson Drive in the summer of 1897. I mind that because it was the old queen's jubilee and I lost my medal up one close and was feart to go back. There was just

ordinary ring-and-run, but if it was a quiet close and you didnae like the woman, you sometimes tied the pull-bell of one house to the door handle across the landing. Then you rang that second bell and skedaddled. You just left the woman to open her door and it pulled the string to the opposite bell . . . many's the time I've wondered what they two women said to each other.

And Duncan White remembers another crime.

There was 'clockwork' too. Easy enough on a ground-floor windie. That was nothing. But we used to fasten the washer wi' the button or the wee screw dangling below it, to tap the pane of a one-up windie. You'd to climb up a pipe to do that. Then you sklimmed back down carrying the long thread and sat behind the wash-hoose to tap-tap the glass. Quite brave mind-you, for if you got caught the woman would hand you a skelp worse'n your own ma, and you neednae bother complain at home for fear of another one.

So for sure, it wasn't all the gathering of rosebuds and cradling dollies folk think of in the childhood of eighty years ago. Bricks in paper bags or under old hats to stub passing toes, string across back courts, squibs in wash-houses. They weren't nice. But maybe that skelp from the clock-worked woman was the answer. Retribution was swifter, less debated and more readily understood, than more careful punishments.

No doubt there were worse villainies but, if there were, the rememberers were loyal to the reputation of their generation, and smiling secret smiles over old devilments, went back to tell of more innocent pleasures.

These were the conkers and rounders and cricket common to most areas, and more local occupations where terrain and landmark called for particular inventions; where the marsh-pond skating of winter gave way to jam jars and tadpoles, where building and demolition sites were littered with see-saw planks and all the other stuffs of adventure playgrounds. There were idling pools on Cart, Clyde and Camlachie Burn, for swimming and fishing.

And there were fields in the old days which seemed to belong to no one but the children who wanted to play there.

> We used to make fires in our field and cook tatties in the embers. D'you mind that tingly black crust you'd to crunch through to get at the white? . . . and we used to cook sausages, and kippers at tuppence a pair (that was about 1937). And then you lay back like old men, puffin' away at your share of a five packet of cigarettes.

But more than anything, then as now, water drew weans, like magnets drew filings.

> I mind the day I fell in the duckpond at Carolside farm. I was leaning over for taddies and I just toppled in . . . came out all green and slimy. My what a mess, and what a reek there was off me. Didnae half get a skelpit leatherin'. Oh dear aye!

That's Mr Noble Boyd's memory of First World War years but when there's an added sin to the draw of water it's irresistible.

> There was a sluice on the River Cart and about September the water was low and we could get over to Lammie's field and scrumpie the apples in his orchard. Usually got our feet all plashing wet as well.

Glasgow children seem always to have been vigorous in their play and street language, and young incomers over the century from Ireland and Italy, Belgium and Poland, and from Jewish communities all over Europe have been quickly absorbed into the mysteries of hets and leave-o. There's always the fear that weans here, as elsewhere, will lose the art of simple play without gear or little miracles of wire and bleep. But it was heartening to hear recently of a gang of youngsters scuffling in a game of tig on a Gorbals street and a skinny red-head shouting to one of his mates from the multi-storey,

> Haw Mahomet . . . you're *het*!

14

CHORES AND NO CHORES

I. MOTHERS AND DAUGHTERS

Scrubbing, polishing, burnishing, clawting out clinkers from coal fires . . . no doubt they're all still done in small endurable doses in Glasgow homes here and there, but surely not often enough to demand of your average weans the regular commitment to them that youngsters in the 1950s and before, knew as their Friday night duty, come what may.

> We'd all wir own chores (just the girls mind). The one week you'd get the manglin', the next the ironin', next help wi' the washing or the brasses or sweep and pipe-clay the front step. Never two weeks the same job. My mother was a wee thin-thin cratur but she took no snash off of us and had us all choopered up to wir jobs.

Of all the tasks doled out to the family, those centred round the fire are the ones best remembered after eighty or more years. Since the first fire-slab was laid under the first lum-hole in a turf roof, the hearth has been the heart of home. It's not surprising that the two words have a common root, for the fire and its tending have been a core memory of every childhood, and living memories of the hearth go back to the days even before ranges were common place.

> My most vivid memory of my granny was seein' her bend over the open fire in her cottage swingin' a swee over the coals and turning scones on a girdle. I didnae think then on the hard, dirty work it was, I just liked the smell!

William Stevenson's mother cooked the meals of his childhood over the fire too.

> We'd no range mind, a range was a kind of luxury, but there was hobs, one each side the hearth, that swung in over the fire.

But for the rest, it was the range, all the way to the 1940s, that was comfort, bane and chore.

> We all congregated, the thirteen of us, in the back kitchen at nights for our high tea. That was from the 1890s. The range was there, and the black kettle on it was never off the simmer. There was a big-big pot of soup aye spitterin' away on the hob too.

And a glowing range with a hissing kettle was a cheerful background to studies, from the days of the 'tupenny' to the college finals.

> We all used to do our lessons, and later on our studying, in the kitchen. It was warm and cheery and if your ma was baking you got a treacle scone or that off the girdle.

But there was a price to be paid for the comfort.

> I mind black-leadin' night. Forbye the range itself to polish, there was a clawt, a shovel, a brush-handle and your open-work fender to be blacked.
>
> Thon range was the scunner of my life. You'd to blacklead it and emery round the steel trims . . . scoor it like daft! My mother wouldnae thole anything less than perfect . . . or maybe less than Mistress Purdie's down the stair . . . but I liked making the toast after, on the end of a fork at the bars.

There were at least the compensations of warmth and toast for the drudgery of burnishing the range but, unless a wean was old before her time there was precious little in polishing the brasses. Certainly not for Helen Stewart, just one of over thirty who claimed Brasso-ing as a major thrall of childhood.

> These brasses, outside and inside, were the bane of my life on a Friday night. My sister got out of that because she had a right genteel job with a florist and she often went out to big posh dos on Friday evenings.

Of course, needs and chores changed with the times and circumstances.

> In the time of the Second World War when I was young it was
> my job to mix the margarine and butter rations, you beat them
> together to give the margarine a wee bit of the butter flavour.
> Spoiled the butter mind, but made the marg better tasted.

Little of the cleaning done in Glasgow at the turn of the century
was by short cut or miracle dust-dissolver and spray. But there were
aids. Throw a 'do you remember?' into a Sunset Home lounge
and you get almost a Greek chorus . . . 'D'you mind Lysol?',
'D'you mind Zebo', 'D'you mind fly-papers?' or Monkey Brand,
or Babbit's Powder or Brooke's Soap? As well as the Lysol and the
Monkey Brand for the fierce cleaning of the house itself, there was
always the struggle for personal freshness. Unlike the view taken
in 1790, by 1890 'clarty' was no longer considered 'cosy'.

Those who had hot water taps at the turn of the century
were not merely keeping up with the Joneses. They *were* the
Joneses. And their bathing facilities were the wonder and envy
of the majority whose arrangements were more primitive.

> This would've been about 1916–17 and in our room 'n' kitchen
> we had the cold but no' the hot. So there was a special bath-night
> . . . Friday night was the *big* night.
> But it was Thursday night the whole caper began. All the
> clinkers and big cinders from the fire got laid aside and the rest
> riddled through to the ash-can for throwin' out. It was that dusty
> too, the whole place! Then the cinders went back wi' new sticks
> and coal for to start the fire up again. When it was goin' nice it
> got banked up wi' dross and let burn low till the next night under
> the big kettles and pots so there was lots of hot water for the bath.
> First though, we'd all our hair unpleated and washed, and Mother
> got out the small-tooth comb and paraffin in case of lice or nits.
> Then the zinc tub came out from under the kitchen bed and one
> after the other we all got our bath.

More explicitly than 'one after the other' Mrs Helen Stewart
describes the ritual in their house.

I had my wash first, in the zinc tub in front of the fire. Then more water was added for Bessie, then Maggie, then John . . . *added* mind. Last one got the rinsings off the rest. By that time around 1916 my bigger brothers had graduated to the tuppenny bath-house in McDougall Street, but we were still in the tin bath. What a job it was, when I think back, to tim the water out that tub.

In another more conservationist house it wasn't always jawed out the minute the last back was scrubbed.

Your ma sometimes used to take the chance to wash through a few clo'es.

But of course it wasn't only weans who steeped themselves at the fire, and the steeping wasn't always private to the family. The daughter-of-the-manse, who was the shy young Sunday school teacher Isobel Cameron, was paying a parish call once in the 1930s.

I was taking a wee prize to a laddie in the Sunday school. He lived in one of the miners' rows for the Cardowan Colliery . . . the rows were a place apart, unique, with names like Heathery Knowe and Maryston. It was my first visit, and I chapped the door.

'Come awa' in, come awa' in,' says the mother, very hospita-ble, ushering me in. And there was her man sitting black as night and quite jokoh, in a big zinc bath in front of a fire that would've roasted an ox, soaping himself ready for her to scrub him. The whole place was festooned with washing and a chair was swept clear of clutter — and the cat, for me to sit down. I ducked the hangings and sat myself there. I was manse mind you, and a bit prim, but they weren't a bit put-out and we just sat there chatting as if it had been my mother's parlour; me and the wife and the tubbing miner.

It was certainly cleanliness that was next to godliness, but not far down the seedings were the other tasks demanded of youngsters in big families if the knit of life was not to fall apart. Eking-out and making-do were prime concerns that give rise to a plethora of chores.

Mr James Ross had a memory of his frugal childhood which he repeated more than once to his daughter Margaret.

When my father was a boy he used to get sent to the fish shop on a Saturday just before it closed when there were bargain prices. He got five pounds of whiting for a shilling and that fish was their Saturday tea and their Sunday breakfast.

And for the Laurie family there was another pet economy.

We used to get sent to Scotland Street, maybe two miles away, to get broken biscuits from Gray Dunn's factory . . . not for visitors mind, just for the family.

The Browns had a recipe for fuel saving . . .

I lived in the Gorbals in the 1920s. My mother used to just half-bake her bread then send us with it like that to the bakery. You got putting it in the big ovens there when the baker was finished his own batches and yet there was still heat in the ovens. Even better, you could take your own flour an' that, and mix your sponges and tea-breads in his big mixers. You used yon big paddles to put things in and take them out the ovens.

Then there was the endless shopping, carrying of rubbish to the midden, chopping sticks and the minding of the wean.

My job was, every day after the school, to take my wee sister, happed in a shawl, out for a bit fresh air in the street. We'd no pram you see . . . no' many had prams in our street, and that was the way she got taken for her walk.

That was William Stevenson's recollection of his place in the scheme of things. But it has to be said that, if the women who look back are to be believed, he must have been almost unique in doing any household duties. There are not many ardent feminists among octogenarian ladies but, almost without exception, their asides about their girlhood chores show how long ago the seeds of protest were planted.

The five of us girls had all our set jobs. One sister did the hall and stair, one the bathroom and two did all the beds. That was before you went to school or work . . . the brothers did *nothing*. They got waited on hand and foot.

That was no gripe-voice in the wilderness. There were plenty more. 'My father *do* anything in the house? Never ever!', 'My father or brothers work in the house? You're kidding!' What an inelegant cry from an 88-year-old gentlewoman! But it was wrung from her by wry memories of long ago injustice. And there's a memory of a health conscious grandfather, born probably around the start of Queen Victoria's reign.

> Our grandfather always stayed in bed on Sundays, in the concealed bed in the kitchen . . . thought he needed that once a week to keep himself fit. We used to visit every Sunday and see him lying in bed. He got his meals and everything served to him there.

And the twinkling ladies who recalled that scene added, 'He was in provisions . . . cured hams', his own included, presumably, after a hard week's work on his feet.

Another husbandly view of his wife's implicit marriage vows to 'love, honour, and run after me' is remembered nevertheless affectionately by a son of the union.

> My father was devoted to his clay pipes, used to break off the stems short so's they would sit comfy in the corner of his mouth, even while he was speaking. Had it in his bed at night too for a last wee puff before sleeping. He smoked an ounce a day easy. But he would never buy his own tobacco. That wasnae a man's job. He used to pass the shop every night and then send my mother out to buy it for him.

And the prize for making all such arrangements possible, goes to the lady who could say,

> Our brother was waited on hand and foot. We'd to clean his shoes and get up early to cook his breakfast. We'd all left school at fourteen and we worked at outside jobs all our lives. But I still think it's a woman's right place to serve the man.

II. FATHERS AND BRETHREN

Well that's the way the women remember it all, but the menfolk have a few rankles too, about what was expected of them by way of carrying coal, emptying ash-baikies, splitting firewood, humphing shopping, and lighting boiler fires on perishing, dark, raw mornings. And Duncan White never knew whether to enjoy his chore when he reached the steamie or die of embarrassment on the way.

> Us boys had to march along the street to the steamie carryin' the dirty washing bundle in the tin tub on our heads. Took turn about on the road there. Then after, we'd get to trample the sheets or blankets in the steamie stall.

Whatever the truth about the household efforts of the menfolk, mothers, grannies, and aunts tend to come across the years as uniformly clever-handed domestic providers, dinning manners and morals, cleanliness and economy, into their children. Fathers, grandpas and uncles, on the contrary, are remembered in fifty different guises of personality, affectionately but, dare it be said, on the whole with marginally less respect. Some were stern disciplinarians of course, but they're credited mostly with telling stories, drawing sweets out of baggy pockets, bestowing pennies and sneaking saucers of creamed butter and sugar to coughing weans, with winking behind the heads of scolding mothers . . . and even sometimes with misbehaving themselves. On occasion there was good reason for Ma's tight lips.

> My father used to come home sometimes quite late from his work, after a wee refreshment. My mother was angry then. Sometimes he used to hide his whisky bottle behind the gas meter in the bathroom. She didnae like that either.

The tenement Saturday night, unlike the Cotter's, was something else mothers often had to bear, and Mrs Edith Dykes feels for hers after nearly fifty years.

> Every Saturday night at tea-time when my father and my brother and my uncle Willie had all been to the same football match, you'd have thought from the argy-bargying of them that they'd all been to different games . . . the rows! It was just a right rammy every week . . . terrible!

And the father who was one of the long-ago arguers is still there to agree and add his pennyworth.

> I could still near tell you the Third Lanark team about that time, there was Brownlie, McCormack, Fairfull . . . I cannae mind the next one . . . but then Fergus, Main, Reid, Sterowski, the Walker brothers and Hillhouse . . . that's no' bad is it?

Fathers, then, came in a wide range. Some, of course, were step-fathers and this one was hardly run-of-the-mill in domestic matters.

> He'd been a cook in the Navy in the First World War. He was English and my mother was Scottish. He used to make rare steak pies and when there was a family 'do' he put a pastry thistle at the one end of the crust and a rose at the other.

Grandpas too had their share of characters.

> I mind of Grandpa Gibson. He kept cough candy unwrapped in a drawer and he used to hand out oosey chunks of it. He was like a wee elf wi' sunk rosy cheeks and bright eyes and he used to take out his teeth to frighten us . . . all gumsy!

Other grandfathers have lived long in the memory, but at ninety-five years old herself, Mrs Henderson recalls not only her grand-parents but her great-grandfather who must have been born around 1790.

> My great-grandpa lived wi' my granny in Uddingston. There's nothin' new, you know . . . them wi' the granny-flats! He'd that in 1894, his wee kitchen and his own room. But then you just called it 'your grandpa stayin' wi' you'. Anyway, he kept a big whip in the corner of his room and if he was angry wi' you for something he used to crack it and threaten you. He'd a staw at m' Uncle Jake and *his* lot . . . no' so much at us . . . but just now and then, aye.

Few remembered fathers came in the Wimpole Street mould. Certainly that whip's crack must have been worse than its lash, for none of the family seems to have been much fashed when it was produced. No word, though, of what Uncle Jake had done to deserve that staw.

15

THEIR WEANS WOULD NEVER BE

I. A GALLUS ADVENTURE

The two wars of 1914–18, 1939–45, were the two great watersheds in the first half of the twentieth century. They were not more traumatic in Glasgow than elsewhere but there were some experiences that were peculiar to the city. Birmingham's wars were Birmingham's wars, Glasgow's were Glasgow's.

But echoes of other wars before 1914 still linger in minds that were young in what we call the First World War.

> I mind my grandfather telling me that he remembered the Crimean War of 1854 and the way they said it was 'General Winter' that was the real enemy and no' just the Russians. He said the sufferin' was that horrible folk thought there could never be another one. Then the Boer War comes along and all the flag-wavin' starts up again. And when he was an old man in 1914 people were singin' and cheerin' theirsel's silly again.
>
> I got taken to see Lord Roberts when he came to Glasgow in 1893 after he was famous in the Indian Wars and the big trek from Kabul to Khandahar. I expected a big giant of a man and here he was just a wee toty man.
>
> There was an uncle in our family that had been on yon terrible march from Kabul to Khandahar about 1880 when nearly the whole Army died.
>
> My brother was born the day of the Relief of Ladysmith in 1900 so they called him George White Henderson after General George White. It was just at the same time too that one of our neighbours got killed in that Boer War.

Then came memories of 1914.

I remember fine the beginning of the First World War. I was about nine years old and there were two things I've never forgotten. It was the end of July and we were away our holidays up at Nigg and there was a German brass band in the village. I can just see them standing playing outside our cottage and collecting money. About two days after that they were rounded up and it was all round Nigg that the police had found maps and charts of the Cromarty Firth stuffed down their instruments.

And the Fotheringham holiday was cut short a few days later when Father was recalled to Glasgow. The family travelled south by train.

I can see this yet too. There was a big Scots Guardsman in the compartment in his scarlet tunic and his kilt. He was away south to join his regiment for going off to France.

A toy-box soldier to a goggle-eyed small boy.

Whether it was true or not that that German band was a group of spies, the north was certainly a sensitive area in wartime. Mr Harry Anderson recalls,

My parents were from Golspie and we always went there on holiday. I remember that in the war my mother had to show a special pass to soldiers at Inverness for us to get any further north.

The Andersons had been in Golspie when war was declared.

I was there at my granny's. The Seaforths came to Golspie to muster and I remember that one of the jam or marmalade companies, maybe Robertson's, very quickly brought out wee cardboard diced Glengarry caps for the children and I remember marching and bobbing along to the recruiting band trying to keep step. All the wee Golspie boys were there wearing their paper Glengarries.

Mr Duncan White has a more sinister memory of the period just before the war, in Glasgow.

My father worked for a German company near the suspension bridge and earlier that year they built a big high new buildin' and I mind the way he used to shake his head. 'The Jerries can see right away-way doon the Clyde from that place. It's no' right. They can see the whole jing-bang of ships and yards on the river.'

But whatever the Germans spied from the suspension bridge or from the charts in their trombones, by August it was all 'on' and the enlisting began.

> I had taken the shillin' to be a Territorial when I was sixteen . . . joined at the hall on Howie's farm-road wi' all my pals in the Auldhoose Thistle footb'll team. We went to Terrier camp at Macrahanish the summer of 1914, came home on a Saturday and were away to the real Army come the Monday. I was in the Argylls and I went to France in the April when I was seventeen.

Others joined the Navy.

> I joined the Navy in 1914 and was sent to a coastguard station at Cape Wrath. But I had been an apprentice blacksmith so I was sent to sea at my own trade, and I was the whole war after that, out east on the cruiser HMS *Blenheim*. It wasnae such a bad life the Navy. We'd good times and I liked sleepin' in the hammock well enough. Five years of it I had. Came out in 1919.

It seemed romantic enough for the girls at home to see their boyfriends ready for glory.

> I was nineteen in 1914, right in that war generation. All the chaps I knew mustered in the local schools and our lot got locked into Cuthbertson Street playground. We used to go round and talk to them through the railings. They were all laugh and chaff then. 'Och we'll be home by Christmas.' Everybody said that.

Those were the very early days when it all seemed a gallus adventure, but by the turn of the year with news of the real war starting to trickle through, it began to turn sour.

> It became the thing to go and see off your friends and relations in the forces leaving the Central Station. The trains were jam-packed as they moved off, the boys leaning out and waving, the wives and mothers standing there singing with tears running down their faces, 'Will ye no' come back again?' I was forever at that station waving off cousins and friends.

Although there was now an awareness at home of the slaughter, only those who were there can suggest the feel and smell and horror of trench war. Mr William Stevenson is one.

I was a machine gunner and the first time I got wounded was in the foot . . . that was the month after I got to France . . . on the Somme. When I was better I was straight back up the line.

After that I think I was in a' the big battles except Loos (it was Kitchener's lot at Loos) but I was at the Somme and 'Wypres' and at Passchendaele . . . what a dirty hole that was, a' glaur and squelchin' mud. I was a private at first, but there were that many gettin' killed that I was a corporal for just five days, then a sergeant at nineteen and a sergeant major at twenty.

I got bad wounded at Amiens when the Germans were tryin' for a breakthrough. I was wounded right through the buttocks . . . no feelin' in my legs and just collapsed . . . lost the use of my legs for a long time and after that I was three-and-a-half year in the hospital.

And Mr Roxburgh remembers his part in the Army's attempt to take the Menin road.

The place was all pitted wi' shell holes and laid wi' mines. We'd to try and follow a tape to guide us through the minefield. But then a shell burst beside me and I got a 'blighty', wounded in the head and neck. The war was over before I was fit again.

But I was lucky by my brothers! The three of them were all killed, two of them under age . . . and my mother was a widow, mind. One of my brothers wasnae found till ten years after the war when workmen on the Menin road found his body buried shallow there, just the week I got married.

For a long time there was little comfort either for those who were having a break from the fighting.

If you'd a few days back from the line there was no canteen nor nothin', no proper beds. You came out maybe in winter in the snow and just put your waterproof sheet on the ground. That was your bed.

But perhaps they did have time during the break for one of the more laborious chores of the kilted troops.

I mind of just sittin' there in perishin' cold behind the lines goin' up and down the pleats of my kilt wi' a match or a lighter to kill the lice that got in there and drove you daft.

Then it was back to the trenches.

At least when it was not seeing action the Navy seems to have been more comfortable for greater stretches of time. And more entertaining.

> We'd a monkey on our ship, and we used to make it drunk . . . used to pour rum on the table and the monkey used to lick it up. Then when it got lively and tried to swing from place to place it used to miss its grip. A shame? Naw, it wasnae a shame, and it wasnae cruel. The monkey thought the rum was lovely.
>
> A lot of the sailors were right keen dancers too, so we just danced wi' each other . . . thought nothin' of it. Then we'd concerts, sailors doin' all sorts of turns, singin' and dancin' and conjurin', and kiddin' on they were winchin' couples in funny sketches.

No doubt there were less happy times for the concert-party tars, as there were for the soldiers. Even at home the authorities were slow to provide even the barest comfort for servicemen in transit.

> I mind of twice comin' into Glasgow late at night. The first time was early in the war and I'd just to sleep on my greatcoat on the station floor. But by the second time, a year later, they'd canvas beds laced up to scaffolding in the station basement, and you got a pillow and a blanket.

So things were moving on the home front and when the first forlorn results of the stunning German advance arrived in Glasgow, the city was prepared to meet them. Twelve hundred Belgian refugees came, first of all to temporary billets made ready in the corporation halls. They came with nothing but what they had worn as they streamed out of their villages, and perhaps a parcel or handbag. Some of them were almost as afraid of the wild mountain people they expected to find living in rough stone dwellings in savage Scotland, as they had been of the Germans. The organiser of the Belgian operation left a diary.

> 1915 Had big 200 gallon tanks of cold water at the station to serve in tin mugs from fifty tea-pots, to give them a fresh drink before sending them off to the various halls where settled and fed. Glasgow

woman in thibet skirt and peenie brought huge barrel of apples to one hall and went round handing them out. One woman refugee had to be rushed to the Maternity to have her baby. Went to London to find small box of belongings she left there. There was much work getting them all settled and billeted into houses and fixed up with clothes and necessities . . .

1919 The king of the Belgians presented me with the King Albert medal.

There was no keeping this kind of war at arm's length in distant places. Information came with brutal starkness.

The thing folk dreaded the most was the casualty lists . . . just sheets and sheets with hundreds and hundreds of names listed in the newspapers.

I was at the boys' high school and every morning at assembly the names of the latest old boys killed were read out, names for the Roll of Honour.

Apart from the droves of women going into munitions, more and more war work was taken on at home. Marie Condie took up nursing.

I joined the VAD. I was young and shy and real shocked when I'd to empty urinals and such, but I got over that when the wounded began to arrive and I'd maybe to work on a laddie with no legs or one with half his face blown away. Later on near the end of the war I went to Bangour hospital when what they called the Big Push was on, and oh my, the terrible wounded that came in on the railway that ran right into the hospital grounds . . . truckloads and truckloads of human wrecks, boys just!

I joined the Woman's Volunteer Reserve under Lady Cargill. We drilled like soldiers in the drill hall at Butterbiggins Road and after the drill and maybe a pep talk, got detailed to go on different duty rosters. You'd canteens for a week or two and then maybe collecting wastepaper.

There were other less worthy activities.

A lot of nasty things went on, profiteerin' an' that, but the worst was when silly women seen you in the street in your civvy clo'es, maybe just on leave, maybe no' in the Army for some reason, and handed you a white feather for a coward.

There's a rag-bag of recollections too, of taking part in fund-raising concerts, selling war bonds from tanks in George Square, the rounding up of Lord Derby scheme recruits by officials with brown armbands, marathons of knitting, endless queues.

> There was a real shortage of a lot of things before they brought in the rationing. You'd to stand in line for tea and sugar and bread and meat. One particular day, for some reason, stands out in my mind. I'd be about ten and I stood for two solid hours outside Kate Young's fruit and veg shop for two pounds of potatoes. Then I remember that we used to get extra sugar so that the rhubarb we grew wouldn't go to waste.

Tobacco and drink were short too and men complained that their beer was watered down. The rueful complaint going the rounds was that the dire lack of liquor could be clearly detected at normal peak drinking times . . .

> It's Saturday night and there's nobody drunk on the tram.

Another fleeting recollection of 1915 was the swift passage through wartime Glasgow in a bleak week of smirring drizzle and gloom, of an exotic party of Canadian Indian troops commanded by Chief Clear Sky. They were on their way to the war and sampled Glasgow hospitality enjoying a first, and no doubt last, taste of black pudding.

> But they left one young Indian behind. His name was Gay Flier. He was very very ill with flu and he died in Govan Military Hospital. My grandpa had been seeing to Chief Clear Sky's men when they were in Glasgow and so's not to let the boy get buried in an unmarked grave he claimed the body and saw to it that there was a right funeral in Glasgow with magistrates there, a gun carriage and a party to fire a salute at the grave. It wasnae among his own open-air folk but it was better than being not heeded at all.

Comments and memories about wartime politicians and leaders are few but the two big Ks were passingly mentioned.

> Everyone knew Kitchener's face fae yon pointing poster and it was a terrible thing when he got drowned. It would've been like Churchill gettin' killed in the next war.

The Kaiser was never such an ogre or wicked bogeyman as Hitler. There was a kind of sneakin' disappointment that one of the old queen's grandweans had turned out so bad and been against Britain, just a dozen years after she died.

Mrs Nancy Watt has a memory of an odd little dispensation granted, even encouraged, at her church in Govanhill.

I remember sitting in the pew during the war at Sunday services knitting white balaclavas for troops fighting where there was snow.

Eventually it was over and not a soul among the rememberers but recalls precisely where he or she was at the moment of Armistice, from mixed infant to veteran soldier.

I was just a wee lassie at the school and the Room 2 door got chapped. Miss Craig went and spoke to another teacher and came back in, greetin'. I never saw a grown-up greetin' before . . . but here she was just happy! After, we went on a peace outing and got Armistice medals.

I was at the high school then and we'd got word to listen for the kirk bells. We were all hanging out the windows in Elmbank Street and when the bells rang out we just rushed out the school and away up Sauchiehall Street, swept along in the crowd.

Another boy remembers school boaters and caps spinning across the heads of stampeding people and getting trampled to nothing under running feet.

Office girls went mad too.

It was indescribable . . . amazing hoardes of douce wee Glasgow folk singing and dancing, shouting, kissing and hugging total strangers. It was quite late when I walked home across the bridge to the south side and there were still folk careering about with wee Union Jacks stuck in their hats. Don't know who thought on having the wee flags ready.

But as the saying goes 'there's aye someb'dy isn't there?' That was at home. For the serviceman it was all more sober . . . well, perhaps not 'sober', but at least less euphoric. Duncan White was aboard the *Blenheim* . . .

On Armistice day I was sailing up the Dardenelles. We celebrated by splicing the mainbrace. That was getting an extra tot of rum. The monkey? I suppose he got the lickin's too. And that was it . . . wi' a wee bit cheerin' and the flags up.

William Stevenson of the Argylls:

I was in the hospital on crutches at that time. I'd gone into the town wi' a friend from the Coldstream Guards. Everyone was going daft huggin' and kissin' in the street and makin' a fuss of the likes of us in our blues. But it was all that much, we just got on the tram and went back to the hospital. It was quiet there.

Two postscripts sum up the forlorn waste of that decimating war.

It was horrible, but you didnae realise the awfulness until you came back looking for your friends again and more'n half of them just werenae there; and their weans would never be.

In 1914 we'd been eight in our house. By 1918 my three brothers were killed and my father and grandmother had died. Now there were just the womenfolk left at home, me, my ma and my wee sister just turned eight.

There's also a third postscript that tells of the tempering of boys into warriors over the years when they should have been learning their trades, playing carefree games and wooing their girls. This postscript is left almost to the end because that's how the old man spoke of it, as an afterthought when the reminiscing was done and it was time to go home. He pointed to a shelf in his room.

That's my things there. That's my DCM (there's a wee pension wi' that) and that's my Military Medal and my Bronze Star. Aye . . . read them if you want.

'I wish to congratulate Sergeant W. Stevenson on the gallantry displayed by him on 31 July and 1 August 1917.' 'I wish to congratulate Sergeant-Major W. Stevenson on the gallantry displayed by him on 21 March 1918.'

He puts the medals back, and the next person to handle them will be the chirpy lass in Eastwoodhill House who keeps them polished for him.

II. THIS AND OTHER ROUGH WAYS

All these memories still haunt those who speak of them after seventy years and perhaps some are blurred a little in hindsight. But among the rest were the recollections of one who was part of a band of bonnie fechters whom no one else had even mentioned, the servicewomen of the 1914–18 war. Extracts from her diary deserve their own space, for its entries are not blurred by tricking memory. They are not spoiled by what she *should* have said, or *wished* she'd said. Young, fresh and immediate, lit with unconscious humour and irony they tell of her first days as a recruit, aged eighteen.

> There was me, with two brothers and a nice boyfriend having a terrible time in France, so I decided to join the WAACS. It certainly wasn't for the glamour of the uniform I can tell you, because we'd just a shapeless coat dress and a wee pork-pie hat that pulled down to your eyebrows.

Later she moved from posting to posting, mainly in transport administration in the Royal Flying Corps, and ended the war in the much smarter outfit of the newly formed WAAF. But it was in the very first weeks of her training that Nancy Reid kept her little journal. She recalls, first, the basic rules.

> Members (of the WAAC) must not alter shape of hat. Any girl who disregards this, will be required to purchase a new one at her own expense.
> Members must discard all jewelled haircombs and ribbons and all jewellery except signet or wedding rings, and address all administrators as 'Ma'am'.
> Members must behave in an orderly manner at all times.

In spite of the holocaust in France, the filth and lice attending the nice boyfriend and brothers in the trenches, she writes,

> One fact which shocks us is that there is no cover on the dining-table here. Had some of the girls known about this and other rough ways I guess the number of recruits here would not be so many.

After roll-call we reported for our first lessons in forming fours . . . two deep etc.

For dinner we had a small piece of boiled mutton, one potato and a little rice without milk. One of my room-mates, a rather fragile affair, hasn't got into the way of eating in the Army. She is very particular about her food and a girl of that sort is *absolutely no use here*. We can only leave her alone until she eats what is put to her, dainty or otherwise.

And an item that in a later age might have been headed, 'Don't let's be beastly to the administrators':

When an administrator enters, everyone is silent and stands to attention. This is really very nice to see because all the officers are extremely nice and deserve a little appreciation. So it is good to have such rules because some would never dream of having any esteem for those in higher rank. The least we can do is lessen their burden by being well-behaved and orderly.

I had a letter from Mamma today and brightened up wonderfully. I seem to see a fire in my bedroom in Chisholm Street and a table set with everything good for eating.

Salt is very scarce here and when we were in a fish restaurant in town Sally pinched a little to save it for a rainy day.

Supper . . . good old soup, alias hot water!

16

SHRIVELLED LIVERS AND LIVE WORMS

We were always teetotallers in our house so we got sent to the Band of Hope. I signed the pledge, och as many times!

That was in the 1890s and the Band of Hope was just as popular twenty years later in the time that James McLachlan was a regular pledger.

It was a great thing on a Friday night, the Band of Hope. They showed you shrivelled-up livers and live worms curlin' up, demented and suffering, in jars of alcohol.

Of all the people remembering for this book, who were young from the 1880s to the early 1930s, only one solitary soul was not a member of the Band of Hope, in some Glasgow church hall or back-room somewhere. Its aim was simple . . . to bolster youngsters against the temptations of liquor abuse in a city scourged and sick with drunkenness. For most secure bairns it represented no more than a worthy activity encouraged by sensible parents; like Sunday school, cleaning the brasses and practising the piano from Hemy's Tutor . . . but one that, for the most part, was fun.

The baldie truth was, you went to get entertained, to have a good night out wi' friends.

admits James Shaw of Cardonald.

The earliest first-hand memories of the Band of Hope are Margaret Henderson's of the 1890s, when the young world of

Uddingston flocked to its meetings in the church hall.

> You got talks and lanterns and a bag wi' a cookie-bun and a cake, and maybe an orange at the swarry. Everybody came to the Band of Hope in our church hall. And we signed the pledge . . . as many times . . . aye dozens of times.

And the same pattern of nourishment for body and soul was repeated on the fringes and in the heartlands of the city, alike.

> I was in the Band of Hope before the First World War. You sang temperance songs on ordinary nights and got buns and tea at the swarries in the Mission Hall near Cumberland Street; and you used to slosh your tea on the floor so's to make slides. We liked the swarries and the magic lantern and we liked Big Dick, the man in charge. I signed the pledge, we a' signed the pledge . . . many's the time.

A real good night out for most youngsters, but for others the Band of Hope was the start of a lifelong commitment to temperance.

> I chanted wi' the rest . . . this would be 1913 or so . . . 'Wine is a mocker, strong drink raging. Whoever is deceived thereby is not wise . . . ' and I just signed up wi' all the others. It was nothin' to me then really, bar a rare night out. I liked the Sunday school, but I liked the Band of Hope better wi' the lantern and the swarries and throwin' your sweeties at the girls. D'you mind them sweeties you used to could buy . . . readin'-sweeties wi' words on them . . . 'Be my rosebud' or 'Can I walk you home?' But all the same somethin' must've got across, for there's still a wee voice inside minds me of the Band of Hope and I never took to drinkin' wine or beer or that. And I'm no' sorry.

For yet others the Band of Hope had a very different appeal, street waifs who counted the days between meetings, with longing.

> For a few hours' warmth and comfort inside a decent building . . . just that once in the week.

That's what one grandfather told his grandson of his very young days in the 1850s.

> He told me that he minded standing as a wee laddie outside a pub on a cold night with his bare feet in his bunnet to keep them

warm, while he waited on his father to come out and give him a penny to get him a bed for the night in a common doss-house.

It was small wonder that bunnet boy hankered to join the Band of Hope, and he hung about the meeting place wishing he had the penny needed to be a real, pledge-carrying member. His grandson goes on . . .

> Then his widower father married again. He set up in a bare tene-ment room and young Wattie thought life had taken a turn for the better. But here the new stepmother was a bit drouthy too.

The night the boy came home at last to show off his pledge-card that some kindly man had bought for him, the woman was sitting half-tipsy in the kitchen. She laughed at him for his pledge, tossed his card in the fire, and when he protested threw a plate at his head.

> He jouked it then he ran out the house to a brother's place and he never set foot in his father's home again . . . he must have been about nine year old then, my grandpa.

But now that young man was in the Band of Hope, pledged and set on course. He learned his texts at the meetings, won a book, taught himself to read and, over the years of self-discipline and improvement, left bunnet and doss-house far behind: but not so far that they were ever forgotten, and during the First World War when he was discussing with Andrew Bonar Law the possi-bility of urging the troops to sign similar pledge-cards (at least for the duration of the war) he had a wry smile at the memory of the barefoot laddie warming his feet in that bunnet half a century earlier.

Not everyone was as alert to what he was doing in the Band of Hope as that earnest member. Eighty years after his pledge, little Nellie Edgar made hers.

> I just loved the Band of Hope. You started off each meeting chantin' the pledge. I was just wee but I chimed in as clear as a

lintie wi' the rest. I didnae quite understand how Provost Gray of our wee burgh came into it, or the girl in my class that was called Isa Beveridge but I fair enjoyed saying that pledge and it gave a right rousin' start to the night . . . 'I agree, with the help of Provost Gray, to abstain from all intoxicating liquors, Isa Beveridge.' Why she signed off I really didn't know till I learned the right pledge when I was a little bigger. 'I agree, wi' the help of promised grace, to abstain from all intoxicating liquor, as a beverage.'

That principle and the pledge, were the bones and stomach of the Band of Hope, but there were all the extra-mural delights as well.

We got rare lantern shows wi' stories about strong drink and drunken fathers and poor wee Nellie sittin' bein' hungry in the corner. But the swarry was the great thing. You got your poke wi' a bun an' a cake an' your biscuit.

Sometimes there was a concert as part of the soirée and those youngsters with talent, or just nerve, did 'turns', reciting heart-rending story-poems, old Scots songs and innocent, romantic ballads. There must have been shy weans at the meetings but the rest jostled for places on the programme, parts in a play maybe or solo spots. And the Band of Hope in its heyday was well known to be a breeding ground for popular performers who grew up to entertain Glasgow in concert parties in the city's public halls. But in young days the church hall was glory enough.

It was Faither always got us ready for the swarry, specially us girls. He used to pleat our hair after its wash-night and leave it tight-screwed-up for a week to get a' ripply for the concert. Sometimes after the week we were more like Zulus than th' angels we were s'posed to be. But we thought we were just the last word when we stepped out on to that platform. After, my mother learned to do rag curls and they were a *lot* more flattering. Faither missed doing the pleats just the same.

Most young people who attended the Band of Hope were happy enough to humour their leaders by obligingly signing the pledge as often as the forms were produced. But not everyone did. From around 1910 Miss Jean Thomson remembers . . .

> We all signed the pledge-card . . . all but David Kirk. He would-nae sign, and that was funny really, because he was right serious David Kirk . . . thought about it a lot. Maybe he had the second sight or something, for, even though he was a very abstemious man when he was up, the queer thing was, he went to work for Johnnie Walker's.

There's a patronising twinkle about most memories of the Band of Hope and it's easy to mock at the ongoings there with the shrivelled-up livers, the readin'-sweeties and the concerts. But there was a fair bit of laughter at the time, at the meetings themselves, and maybe the worthy men and women who gave up their time to run them, unconsciously knew a thing or two about psychology and had the right way of it.

> They were a bit kind of psychy I think . . . knew how to put it over, so's that you minded things as were rousin' and funny, better'n long-faced teaching.

And from his own memories James McLachlan agrees . . .

> You dinnae easy forget the way they used to could put a wee pinch iron filings on a saucer of burnin' alcohol and show you them goin' red-hot and sparkin' up . . . it was s'posed to be a dreadful warnin' all that, about what went on inside of you, if you drank.

17

BOILER, STEAMIE AND GREEN SOFT SOAP

Mary MacKenzie came to Glasgow as a child from the clear light of the Highlands in the summer of 1898. At home in fair weather they had still taken their clothes in boynes to the peat burn for soaping, slapping and syning in the running water. Before she came to Glasgow one of the tales told her was that the women there still lit fires on the Glasgow Green and heated water in baikies to tub their washing, and that all over the green on winter afternoons there would be the dying lights of fires flickering low in the gloaming.

> I didn't believe that any more'n I believed that the streets were littered with gold. But I did think there might be pumps and wells and a lot of carrying of water up the close-stair to do the washing in the houses.

Glasgow was grey and dreich to Mary MacKenzie but she came to love the wee warm stone-built wash-houses she found in the back greens of the tenements.

Glasgow wasn't all tenements, but even the inner-city cottages and rows, as well as the bien villas on the outskirts, had their washing-houses attached beyond the kitchen. But whether the wash-tubs were in the back-courts or butted onto the houses they were all much-of-a-muchness for fittings and had all the banes and bonuses of wash day in common.

In the early days of living memory, two round, iron-hooped wooden tubs with handles sat on a long low table in most wash-houses. There was a safety-plank nailed to front and back, because a tub of hot suds on a table slittered with soft soap could be lethal. A cold water tap was set into the wall and an iron boiler, built round with brick or stone, sat over a fire-place. There was a 'dolly' and dolly-barrel for dumping out the grime and sometimes a big mangle in the corner.

The ritual began early, winter and summer, with someone going down to fill the boiler and kindle the fire under it. Most of the family took a turn at that chore. Most of them, but not all.

> My mother sometimes, or maybe me or yin of my brothers, we a' took wir turn . . . except of course my faither. It wasnae his place to do things like that.

Mary Hardy remembers the next part of the timetable.

> When the water was hot and there was a good steam-up in the wash-house, whoever was to do the washin' (mostly the washer-woman) went away down the stair and disappeared for the whole morning. Some of the hot water was jawed into one of the tubs and some left for boilin' the whites that had been steepin' all night to loosen the dirt . . . Then everything boilable was boiled.

The rest was pummelled by the dolly and if there was a spare child in the back-court it was conscripted for the mangling. Eventually the washer, with a face red as a winter sun, emerged to hang up the clothes on the green or upstairs on the kitchen pulley, or perhaps set them up in front of the fire on a winter-dyke.

> But it wasnae aye just your clo'es that came out clean fae the wash-hoose, for many's the time, after the washin' was done, there was still a good boilerful of water that had taken a bonnie penny to heat, and your ma couldnae think to waste. So she kep' an eye on it till the boilin' heat was off it then she used to get us in fae our peevers or peeries, strip us and gie's a good latherin' in the suds. After that her week's shot of the wash-hoose was done.

When the high tea was over and the dishes washed, the wise and far-seeing of the grown members of the family had pressing en-gagements elsewhere, while the foolish virgins found themselves caught up in the ironing. The flat irons lay on the kitchen range, two or more of them to keep the work going.

> You could get quite a heat up on them mind and you used to lick your pinkie and just tip the iron and if there was a wee sizzle, it was ready. Ma's rough sheets that she got for her weddin' (that was 1882) were the worst. Too dry and you couldnae get them smooth, too wet and your iron just stuck, and crumpled them as bad's ever again.

Well-ironed clothes were a matter of pride, not only for the ironer, but for the wearer.

> Oh you got your orders right enough, from them all. 'See and get they cuffs right Annie. You cannae be slip-shod about the cuffs.'

A dead metaphor, odder than the simple reminder . . .

> Mind my sash for the swarry Ma.

or a dapper father's requirement.

> My father was a right wee toff . . . used to want his bootlaces ironed.

By the early 1900s the tubs in the washing-houses were plumbed in, and there were wooden sinks with sloping fronts for comfortable standing and a good rasping angle for the washboard. Fifteen years later in newer buildings and the kitchens of genteel villas, the tubs were white wally. But the coal-fired boiler was still to the fore.

Even in areas of congested living there was pride in the job well done and old, trusted and faithful aids to the decent line of suds were carted downstairs every wash day.

> There were eighteen families to our block, six houses to a landing . . . a room-and-kitchen and two single-ends at each side . . . three storeys, eighteen families. When it was Mother's wash day and the water was steamin' in the boiler, she'd get away down there wi' her board and her packet of Co-operative AI washin' powder (none of your fancy biological this-or-that, mind). And aye, she always had her Windsor soap for scrubbin' and dolly-blues for the table covers and pillowcases.

By about 1915 the ironing was done with a bolt iron, its red-hot slab inserted from a cleek through a slot in the back of the iron. And a year or two later in houses with gas-rings at the range, there were gas-irons. The job was done on the kitchen table, the jets inside the iron fed through a tube from a tap at the range.

The names of first teachers, favourite concert turns, family doctors and local characters trip off the tongues of eighty and ninety year olds so readily that when many of them remember, just as easily, various washerwomen of their childhood it must surely have been that they were women of unforgettable personality. They were also, of course, of prime importance to the decent survival of the family . . . Cathie McMillan's family anyway.

> I mind Molly Stevenson, she came to wash. It was a great day . . . wash day. I can smell the suds yet. I used to like that smell . . . washing-soda it would be, likely. My mother didn't think Molly Stevenson was very good at the washing, but she put up with her for fear of having to do it herself.
>
> I mind of Bridie Traynor. It was the way she spoke! We had a friend called Miss Connell when I was wee, and once when I heard Bridie ask ma for a caun'le to light the wash-house, I must've rankled that round in my mind for a while, then I asked ma. 'Is Miss Connell's right name Beatrice *Candle*?'

It was hard work, but there were perks for the washerwomen too.

> We'd an Irish one, Mrs Monaghy. She came every week. The hot water and the green soft soap would be ready for her and she got a tot of whisky before she started. Then she got her dinner and another tot afore she went home.

Some preferred a longer drink.

> Our Daisy Watson aye started wash day wi' a Wee Murray out the kitchen press.

The washerwomen had their side to it all too, of course, and they had sometimes to come to terms with their ladies. There was a general belief among those 'ladies' that it kept the 'women' on their toes, to have to re-do work occasionally, just on principle. Violet Tomkin's grandmother was one such 'woman'.

> My granny used to go out washing. One of her 'places' was a posh house in Jordanhill. She got half-a-crown for a day's work (this would be about 1922). She was a real worker my granny, and a rare washer, and so she was awful insulted when the mistress came out one day and looked at the washin' on one of the lines.
>
> 'I think that stretch could do with another wash and dolly-blue, Teenie.'
>
> Now my granny wasnae a young woman. She'd a hard life, lost a son an' a grown-up daughter and now she was rearin' *me* up. She looks at the washin' . . . 'It was a lovely washing Hen, so it was,' she told me when she came home.
>
> But she needed the work and so she just nodded to that Mistress Eadie.
>
> 'I'll just hang out this pile first,' says my granny. The mistress comes back later from her afternoon at some tea-party. The washin's done and there's my granny synin' round the sink, and the clo'es all out blowing an' billying on the line just as clean's the madam had left them.
>
> 'That's better Teenie. What a difference with the extra run-through and the dolly,' says she.
>
> And my granny just says, 'Aye.'

Although that granny did her scrubbing in the back wash-house, the days of wash-houses were numbered. But there's just a last minding of their hey-day when one wean could still say, with venom, to another, as an even deadlier insult to its mother than impugning her morals.

> *Your* mammy *smokes* in the wash-hoose!

Whether the taunt suggested that only a slattern would breathe tobacco or spill dog-ends among the new-washed clothes or that the very act of lighting-up in secret tokened a woman who was no better than she should be, the rememberer would not tell, and the answer is buried in the rubble of the derelict back-court washie.

The days of solitary rub-a-dubbing were nearly over since by then Glasgow had built its chain of public baths and wash-houses, and brought revolution to wash day. Revolution and a new social divide. The steamie had arrived.

Ladies did not go to the steamie, but those who did found that it had its own culture and chaff, from which the toffs were never missed. The steamie was divided into stalls, each with its small iron boiler and sink, let out at a shilling an hour.

> If we werenae there to help her carry the wash-bundle to the steamie, Ma used to put it in a zinc bath and tie it to an old pram, then push it there hersel'. But many a time I was there wi' her, to tramp the sheets or blankets or just help her to manhandle the clo'es. I mind there was an iron dryin' rack called a horse. It was a long thing and you pulled it out, put your clo'es on it and then pushed the whole lot back into a kind of quick-drying chamber. And there was another thing forbye that, a sort of hand-cawed drier. There was a man there did that. You draped your washin' on a frame, he birled it round wi' the handle and all the wet came spinnin' out the clo'es.

It was during that break when you were getting your tuppence-worth of the drying that there was time for a bit of clash with neighbours and friends. There at the steamie, women whose homes were too small to entertain visitors enjoyed an alternative social life . . . in winter it was warmer and brighter than the street, where they hobnobbed and heard the bruit of the district in spring and summer.

> Oh aye, the steamie was warm, and on cold days it drew you like a poultice.
>
> I was twenty-one when I got married and went away to live, over 300 yards from my mother, the other end of the village. I was terrible hame-sick because I didnae know the neighbours. Be-sides, though I had a nice house (red sandstone wi' a wally close) there was no hot water. At first I went to my mother's to do my washing, but then I heard women talking about the steamie and all the jokin' and gossip that went on. 'Nellie,' says I to myself, 'you're missin' a lot of fun, no' goin' to the steamie.'
>
> So I booked a stall and in I went, I was that green and stu-pid I didnae know I had it for just the one hour. I thought it was

mine till my washin' was done, so I didnae hurry up. Here was me, thinkin' it was nice to be a grown-up married woman washin' at the steamie, when two big irate women descended on me and gave me lalldy for goin' over my time. Well, here's me wi' my wee iron boiler boilin' away good-o, and I didnae know how to get my things out quick. So I yanked it out best as I could and slittered it trailing away, to get dried off a bit for takin' home. I never had the nerve to go to the steamie again.

The next change in washing arrangements came with the rash of new housing schemes . . . those marvel-homes with four rooms forbye the kitchen and bathroom, and set in small enclosed gardens. The steamie was left to the tenement dwellers.

There was a double wally sink, a shallow side and a deep. And there was a grand galvanised gas boiler in the kitchen that stood on wee bowley legs and had a gas ring under it. I'd never seen anything so labour-saving in my life. You could do your washing in your own two tubs wi' the boiler lid plopping and shushing there in your own kitchen . . . and any day of the week. That was a real treat after the wee cafuffles you used to have, up the close, over the head of the wash-house.

And something even more labour-saving than the magic boiler was on its way, to the Watt household, anyway, very early in the gadget's history.

My husband won a money prize from his employers and decided to install a washing machine. It was the wonder of Clarkston for it must've been one of the very first in the neighbourhood. It had a rotary action and friends used to come in and watch the things birling round, and even bring wee bundles of their clothes to get them done for them . . . very sociable really.

Just like the steamie in fact. But private, and in Clarkston.

The novelty of gawping at someone else's washing machine soon wore off. Indeed the greatest boon it was offering before long was that you didn't have to watch it at all, and you could do six jobs on wash day instead of just one. What started the mid-century years as a decadent indulgence soon became as necessary to a young working bride as her wedding ring. Built-in spinners and driers even threatened to kill off pulleys . . . although many a sensible household has since rediscovered the usefulness of the old 'pole'.

With that mention of the pulley, let the chapter end as it began, with another Highlands lass come south. She went into service in Pollokshields, intelligent, but new to the sophistications of city life. During the girl's first week the mistress of the house went into the kitchen to find her new maid perched on top of the step-ladder carefully draping the washing over the pulley, quite unaware that the contraption could be let down.

And if you like a happy ending . . . that girl learned quickly, and about more than pulleys. She occupied her walking-out time to good purpose and subsequently married a Pollokshields gentleman. In time she was, no doubt, able to put some other naive girl wise to the ways of her own kitchen equipment.

18

ROTHESAY WAS THE BIG-TIME

Until the turn of the century a day off work in July was as much as most ordinary folk could expect for their annual holiday. They might make a round of the fair on the Glasgow Green, take a walk to either the Queen's Park flagpole or the high point of the Necropolis to see the strange sight of their city, smokeless, while its factory chimneys were at rest. Some with a little money put by took a 'shillin'y' evening cruise from the Broomielaw, listened to the German band on the paddle-steamer and saw the villages beading the edges of the Firth of Clyde. Perhaps that was what started them dreaming, or gave them big ideas.

Actually, as always, it was the top-drawer folk who started the drift to the Clyde coast for holidays, by building second homes with vistas up the sea-lochs and across the scattering of hilly islands.

One who saw himself at his seaside mansion as a host of real distinction and flair was Mr Tom Watson's grandfather, Walter Freer (noted elsewhere as the blaefoot laddie warming his chapped feet in his bunnet). By the years of the fine coast-house he was a man of wealth and consequence, known to many as 'Mister Glasgow' himself.

> My grandpa bought a big place at Saltcoats and he used to have weekend parties there. He'd horses in his stables for his guests and all-his-orders, but it's the invitations he sent out that I mind as well as anything. There used to be a note at the bottom of each card . . .
>
> 'Train with special saloon carriage attached, leaves St Enoch Station Glasgow at 2p.m. for South Beach Station.'

The fashion was now set by the likes of Walter Freer. Bien folk began to copy biener, in this fancy for real holidays, sleeping in other people's homes: and your ordinary wage-earners took to the whole idea like ducks to water . . . literally water, for the Clyde in all its glory was on their doorstep, with small towns and clachans set in sandy bays, ready made for every taste and pay-poke. The coast and island folk themselves discovered that the sea could bring them more than fish and seaweed, and they began to cater for their city neighbours' new whim.

> My grandfather was piermaster at Kirn at the time the big houses were being built down the Firth of Clyde. He could see that wealthy folk were beginning to rent out these houses for holidays when their owners werenae using them. So Grandpa says to himself why should ordinary folk no' come their holiday as well, if they could get wee places to stay. Well, he'd a good bit money put by, so he built a nice tenement block at Kirn and began to let out the houses for a week or a fortnight to just plain folk from Glasgow. Then he put up a row of shops for them too. Kirn thought itself a cut above Dunoon mind, and the Kirn folk were angry at Grandfather to start with. But they soon got used to the idea and were letting out their own rooms. Later he built a whole lot of wee summer houses for letting on the ground behind his own cottage. His name was Brown, so they called his place Broon's Back.

Glasgow in these heady days was boom city and the boats were coming down the river packed with summer visitors, the menfolk often commuting morning and evening.

> I mind Kirn pier when it was black wi' jerry hats night and mornin'. Jerry hats were kind of high bowlers like chamber pots.

That was Broon and those were the visitors he provided accommodation for, ninety-odd years before. Other hosts, with only their homes to rent out, squeezed themselves into their back kitchens and let every other inch to Ma, Faither and the weans from Glasgow.

The Edgars from Pollokshaws were ahead of their neighbours when it came to getting away for more than just a day trip.

We were one of the first families round our way to have regular holidays. Oh my, but you should just have seen the washing and ironing and packing to get the eight of us ready for off! We used to take our Japanese hamper . . . yon soft kind of woven straw like potato baskets. It started off flat when it was empty, then, when you piled in the coats and towels and sheets, the sides came up higher and higher. The lid was deep as well so that packing could go away above the rim of the bottom part. The very first holiday we had was at Saltcoats. My mother took a house for a fortnight and I mind the other kids standin' at the close-mouth and chantin' when we were going away . . .

'Gooo — d ridd — ance tae baaa — d rubb — ish!
Gooo — d ridd — ance tae baaa — d rubb — ish'

In the earliest years of holidays, the Clyde coast resorts remained mainly the quiet communities they had always been, but as the seasons came and went, each one acquired the personality and characteristics of the clientele which came back year after year. Largs, Saltcoats, Dunoon, Rothesay and Helensburgh were the big-time, with dancing, entertainers, pubs, cafés and souvenir shops, while in the quiet hamlets round the Gareloch and Strone, Skelmorlie and West Kilbride, you found your own amusement. Memories of one style are as much cherished as those of the other.

But before enjoying the charms of the chosen venue you had to get there. Part of the excitement was the journey itself, whether by train, sailing all the way, or a combination of steamer and rail to add to the adventure and confusion.

It was the train for the young Wotherspoons.

When we went to Maidens seven summers in a row, before the First World War, we went by train with three or four hampers and hat-boxes and the high wicker pram in the guard's van.

It was sailing for the Whites. On the paddle-steamers the crew seem to have been pretty eechy-ochy about the amount of the fare, depending on the whim of the man who collected the money.

> We used to go to Ro'say and I mind one time we were all sittin'
> (the eight of us) in a row on one of them long slatted seats. Along
> comes the man in the cap and looks at us all. He jerks his head to
> my father.
> 'They a' yours?' says he.
> 'Aye,' says my father, gettin' out his money.
> 'I'll just take it for the hauf of them.'

There was real competition among the private companies that
sailed their paddle-steamers all the way down from the city's
Broomielaw, but many folks preferred to take the train to
Gourock, Wemyss Bay, Largs or Ardrossan and then the shorter
sail to the holiday place. The Big Three railway companies, the
Glasgow and South-West, the Caledonian, and the North British
all had their own steamers meeting the trains, and competition
among these three was notorious. Although one steamer could
have taken all the passengers on a particular trip, there would be
three sailings perhaps no more than fifteen minutes apart.

The holiday let was by now usually for a month . . . a
month's holiday for Mother and the younger weans, with Father
and the older ones taking their week or fortnight and joining
them for the weekends.

> Mother used to take this wee house at Ro'say. There was Willie,
> myself, Rachel, James, Robert and Emma; the young ones went
> wi' her, but Father and them that were workin' or goin' wi' milk
> or papers didnae get down till the weekends.

That was the pattern, and for some, holiday time off at all was a
generous perk of the job, for others it was a sacrifice.

> When we'd our holiday it was just a wee-wee house we took and
> Faither came for a week . . . a week mind . . . wi' no pay.

Meeting Father was one of the holiday highlights.

> We used to go down the Clyde and up to a wee clachan near Invera-
> ray for a month. Father came at the weekends by horse charabanc
> over the Rest-and-be-Thankful from Helensburgh.

Father used to take the train to Craigendoran, then up the West Highland line to Garelochhead at a shilling for the whole journey. We used to go and meet him at tea-time on Saturdays.

So now they're all settled in their cottages, rooms and farm-houses up the Kyles of Bute, or along the Clyde coast and its sea-lochs: and the roaming and explorations begin that are to be fondled in the memory for ninety years.

There were the laid-on excitements that were a revelation to little girls like young Miss Janet Macleod, from douce homes with strict fathers . . . fathers for the moment safely at home making the family pennies.

We were usually Whiting Bay people, quiet sedate Whiting Bay . . . but here this year it was rooms with attendance at Largs, and Largs was a milestone for me, for that was the year I discovered the enter-tainers. I had never in all my born days seen anything like them . . . the Alvin Sawyers Troupe, with their dancing and singing, their comic cuts and their chorus. We used to sit in the open air, behind the rows of benches that you paid for, and watch them. They wore white sailor caps and reefer-kind jackets in the day and monkey mess-jackets in the evenings. This was all about 1910, about the time of Alexander's Ragtime Band. I'm sure they played that. I used to sit there with my sisters in the mornings, carried away by Miss Sylvia Watt's singing. Then we couldn't get our dinners down fast enough to get back for the afternoon show, and the same at tea-time.

'What's the good of "attendance"', Ma used to complain, 'if you don't stay long enough to eat what the landlady makes?'

And there were the pleasures of the pier.

I used to like the machines at Ro'say pier. I never ever had much mon-ey for the footballers and the palm-reading machine wi' the wee metal buttons, so I always ended up at yon crane that lifted prizes from a pile of jelly beans. You used to see a watch or somethin' gettin' into its claws and then just when it began to swing over to the chute that sent it out to you, everything except a coupla jelly beans dribbled back down among the rest. But once I got a silver cake-fork that I have yet.

Apart from the entertainers idolised by young holiday-makers, there were sometimes other notable people to be seen at the Clyde resorts.

When I was staying in Rothesay in 1907 I can remember we used to see the Bute bairns, the Marquis of Bute's wee ones, coming along the shore carried in two creel-pannier things slung over a donkey. That's a picture I always have in my mind about Rothesay.

Even in quieter spots there were characters worth seeing, and better adventures in finding them.

We used to take a wee boat across Loch Long and beach it on the shore near a cottage where there was an old man lived. He would've been maybe 98 years old the first year we went, then up to 101 in the next three. It was quite the thing for holiday-makers to go and just *look* at this old chap, sitting outside his cottage selling post-cards of himself as souvenirs.

'How are you the day?' you used to ask.

'Och I'm fine . . . fine, ' says he. Same thing every time. He just made a living out of being 100. He was there for viewing beside his wee house on the shore.

Another quaint house, another yearly visitation by the young Gilmours.

We used to scramble along the shore to visit an upturned boat that was made into a home, a proper wee dwelling-house. The locals used to call it Susie's Castle, and Susie lived there with her man. It was an old Para Handy kind of coal-boat that used to sail the Clyde and they lived there, those, two, like Pegotty, summer and winter with their wee bit garden round them and a path running up behind it to the Garelochhead road. If we hadn't been afraid to go too near we'd maybe have got to see the inside. But it was just enough to go and look at them from a safe distance . . . at the boat with its tin chimney and wee bits of curtain at the port-hole windows and at them sitting outside chawnering and quarrelling all the time, Susie smoking her short clay pipe ('cutty cleys' they used to call those).

Of course it wasn't all as idyllic as that picture suggests . . . it never is.

I mind the local folk used to tell us that they took a terrible lot of drink the two of them, and when they came back from the pub taking the width of the road, they'd just stop at the top of the path, lie down, and roll home to the bottom.

It's difficult for modern folk with gardens, or their cars to whisk them to coast or country in half an hour, to sense the exhilaration of pavement-and-cobble weans, in the openness of sea-shore or green field. In those days, both of these were too many hours, and too much money, away from the city for anything but that once-a-year visit for the holidays . . . it's difficult to understand the love and loyalty a few summers could arouse in such bairns for a holiday place.

> I loved Clynder, we went every year and I knew every chuckie on the Clynder beach.

> Ah Whistlefield! We went for years to Whistlefield. When we stayed at the croft there we knew everyone. We rambled in the hills and up the burns and we helped with the three cows and the hens . . . and then at the haymaking.

> We went to a cousin's cottage near Inveraray. He'd a small boat that we used to sail and when we were old enough we used to take it over to St Catherine's for the village hops and then sail home by moonlight. It was very romantic.

Holidays were never holidays without paddling and bathing, and recollections of costumes stretch from bloomer suits and rubber mob caps, to clinging two-tone cottons with thigh-hugging legs, and on, in the march of fashion, to the man-made nylon ruches and svelte tricels. (There the recorded memories of swimsuits end, except for comments from eavesdropping grandweans who sport bikinis and less, scarcely worth the manufacturer's effort of knotting the thread to stitch.)

Not all the paddlers went down to the water's edge. The sea was brought up to some, sitting Mahomet-like on the prom.

> My aunt always took her family to Rothesay. She was very stout and liked to sit on a bench above the shore. There she used to dispatch her daughters down to the jetty with a bucket for sea water for her feet. Down went the girls and spoke to the boatman, very polite.
> 'Please may we have a bucket of water for Mother?'
> 'Help yoursel's lassies. It's a' free. '

But total immersion was better.

> We went paddlin' and bathing. We'd no costumes or that, and I mind once seein' the boys goin' in, just in their wee breeks and wantin' to do the same. So I just sat down on the sand and wriggled off everythin' but my knickers and went wadin' away in like that. I didnae half get a leatherin' after, for wettin' my knickers.

Then it was time for the last picnic, the last washing of sand from between the toes, the last visit to the entertainers, the last buying of seaside rock, and souvenir hankies with Bonnie Scotland embroidered on them . . .

But there are souvenirs and souvenirs, and not many found one like Mr Alick Murdoch's.

> When I was a laddie I spent all my holidays at Kirn, helping on the pier. And I got to know the steamers and the different wee things about them all . . . every detail . . . I just loved those steamers. Then when I was a man and they were breaking up the old *Iona* paddle-steamer in 1936 I bought the bridge and deckhouse. Had it for a summer-house in my garden for over forty years. When we moved house it had to be lifted by crane over the garden wall to a lorry and taken to the new place. Yon was a grand summer-house.

So while most folk were content to enjoy the Clyde, recreate themselves at its beauty spots and then leave those joys behind, and come home with no more than their sticks of rock, a handful of shells and their memories, Alick Murdoch brought back his bit of the river's life to the city. He was sitting in that deck-house on fine days still, at ninety-four, seeing himself as a paddle-struck laddie on Kirn pier, signalling in the steamers to disgorge the streams of his fellow Glaswegians come 'doon the watter' for their holidays.

19

DOIN' BUSINESS WITH OUR SCRAPS

What do Samantha's computer toy and Jasper's Action Man have in common with Mary's post-card album or Davy's diabolo of long ago? Not much you might think.

And yet for the 100-odd years this book concerns itself with, children's indoor toys and games have been more or less simple answers to seven needs: to collect or compete, to read or to cuddle, to perfect skills, to invent or to revel in games of chance.

Take collecting. Children have ever been magpies. Roman bairns stationed with fathers guarding Antonine's Wall at Milngavie probably amo-amassed legion buttons or helmet feathers; young Mungo may have decorated his cell with chuckies from the Molendinar, and no doubt wee Burrell hoarded broken plate chips before getting into the big league with his first teenage purchase of a painting.

Perhaps the items most persistently collected by the young over the years have been their scraps . . . flowers, baskets of fruit, beautiful ladies, soldiers, little brides and grooms, funny bauchly wee men and babies have all gone in and out of scrap fashion over the years, but throughout all the decades remembered by elderly Glasgow ladies, who once haggled over their exchanges, best cherished and valued have been their beloved angels.

Around 1906 Dorothy Laurie was a far-ben scrap dealer and collector, who kept hers in a Gold Flake box.

The second best things were hands . . . two hands clasped across a map of the world. You got that picture in all different sizes. But the very favourite were your angels. You got a lot of angels . . . all like fat cherubs really. You used to sit at the close-mouth to change them with your friend. 'An angel for a hand' you used to offer, and if it was wee angels you'd to fit three or four of them to a big hand . . . or four–five teenie-wee hands to a big angel . . . to make it fair you see.

They went through the decades cutting up crisp new sheets of angels, hands, Lucy Atwells, Mickeys and Minnies. They hoarded them, scarce and thinning, through two wars, then swapped new ones and pasted them into scrap books through the 1940s and '50s . . . All too innocent a pleasure surely for today, you say to a lady who loved her scraps at the turn of the twentieth century.

That's no' true. I was in the shop this past week just, and there was this wee lassie rummaging through a box of scraps. And you know I could just see mysel' sittin' on the school wall wi' my pal, me wi' my legs through the railings one way and hers the opposite, doin' business wi' our scraps.

An exploratory slip round to the same shop reveals the 1980s taste in scraps, Top Cat, Mister Men, Space-folk . . . and still holding their holy own, sonsy dimpled angels with damp curls and blue wings, swathed in soft clouds.

Scraps were not the only barter-currency, there was silver-paper too and the stamps the brainy boys swopped.

But wi' us it was mostly ciggy-cards. You got them off of some man you seen lightin' up. 'Gaunie gie's yer cigarette-photie, Mister?' you used to say.

And Mister usually obliged without a word.

Collecting post-cards to put in albums wasn't an extravagant pastime either, when you could buy them at twelve for fourpence-ha'penny.

I remember being on holiday at Largs about 1908 or 1907 and buying them at fourpence ha'penny a dozen. The stamps were a ha'penny each so you could send cards to twelve friends for ten-pence ha'penny.

There were novelty shapes in post-cards too.

My very best were the ones that you got in the shape of letters, and people sent you the right ones so's that on the front page of your book you had them arranged in your own name. So I had eleven cards making up . . .

There have always been true originals who hoard the odd things that intrigue and pleasure them particularly, bobbins, thimbles, bottle tops, butterflies, but the post-cards, the scraps, the stamps, the ciggy-cards and the autographs belong to mainstream collecting and are true fashions of the past century.

When you tired for the time being of your precious albums and shoe boxes of treasure, and were ready to pit your wits against a rival, there were games and competitions galore, dominoes, charades, happy families and ping-pong. Shorter-lived crazes were pegotty, lexicon and the 1950s obsession with canasta and Chinese chequers. And for Mr Noble Boyd in his young years around 1912 there was . . . the dreaded cribbage.

My oh my! Was there no' just cribbage in our house? My father deaved us about cribbage when I was young. We spent hours and hours, days and days, months and months . . . *years* playin' cribbage. My father kept a league table all totted up in notebooks. Oh my, that cribbage!

When there was no one else to play with, there was always something to read.

I liked *The Basket of Flowers* and *Helpful Nellie* when I was about nine. Then a bit older, *John Halifax – Gentleman*. But best of all I liked *The Channings* and I used to nearly cry at the bit where young Charley gets his head shaved in the fever. You see I mind it all after seventy years.

Later favourites were *The Scarlet Pimpernel* and *The Wind in the Willows*, but by the 1920s the craze was for adventure with Richard Hannay and the Gorbals Diehards. *The Settlers of Karossa Creek* and the Chippewaya and Athabascan Indians. Ten years later it was *Out with Romany* and wandering the leafy lanes of Prince Edward Island with *Anne of Green Gables*. As well-remembered as any of the books are the magazines and comics that poured out, from *The Quiver* of the old century and the Penny stories of the 1900s.

> My aunt Lizzie had a wee shop in Cumberland Street and she sold Penny books; they were green wi' brown letterin'; fairy tales and adventure stories, and when my hands were clean I got to read them before they were sold.

Playbox, Rainbow, Jingles were staple fare of the 1920s, and ten years later *Little Dots, Mickey Mouse, Film Fun* and the *Dandy* and *Beano*. And there's no generation gap even now, between grannies and their grandweans over *Oor Willie* and *The Broons*. Big boys had *Rover, Wizard, Hotspur,* and *Adventure*, and Frank Richards, who gave them Harry Wharton and Billy Burner, became *Hilda* Richards to bring Barbara Redfern and Bessie Bunter to their sisters. Mrs Colinette Allan remembers them.

> I loved a Friday. I got the *Girl's Crystal* at lunchtime and read it during Silent Reading while the teacher did the register. D'you remember Silent Reading? I don't suppose it was for the *Girl's Crystal* really, though.

And Kate Thomas . . .

> But you couldnae aye be readin' books or playing tiddlywinks. There were times, when you were wee, that it was just your teddy or your doll that you wanted . . . when someb'dy'd stolen your scone or give you a cuff on the ear.

Teddies were perhaps more comforting, but give or take an eye or a chewed ear they have been much of a muchness for general appearance and style since they first appeared. They rejoice in no other names; no other adjective than 'my' was used by any rememberer to describe them; and they were, without exception *he*. The 'I' of the 'my', of course, could be either boy or girl.

Dolls on the other hand ran the whole gamut of styles, came in *hes* and *shes* and had as many different names as their owners who were, until the birth of Action Man, always girls. Mary Hardy remembers her Rosy.

> She had a china face and real hair and she had jointed arms and legs and dainty wee toty fingers. She was dressed in helio satin with lovely petticoats and knickers and she had a hat with a feather. Mind I only got to sit with her when visitors came. She wasn't for what you might call *playing*. I kept her to give to my own wee lassie, but when I took her out, the elastic in her joints was perished and she all fell apart. I was as sad as if I'd been seven.

And the daughter who didn't get the ornamental doll remembers getting another.

> My father won a huge dolly at the Empire Exhibition in 1938, so there was no other name for her but Bella Houston. She'd long, long dangly legs and woolly pigtails, and she'd a tartan tammy and skirt. I loved her till she burst and all the sawdust came out.

Twenty years before that, Betty Laurie had another beloved doll.

> He was a boy doll and I called him Gordon. He had a blueish green furry body and a lovely face, not china but smooth and made of some hardwearing stuff because he lived to be an old man did Gordon. One time I changed him to be a girl right enough (away ahead of the doctors I was, doing that about 1917). But *I* just did it by sticking on some of my own curls that had got cut off when I had sore eyes.

Girl dolls, boy dolls . . . and of course baby dolls, to be petted and crooned over and cradled. Muriel and Margaret of the 1910–14 batch of little mothers remember a holiday house with lace curtains that they could tie up into loops that made perfect, draped cribs. There were other homes of course where it would have been unthinkable to buy a child a doll at all . . . make one of wood, or knit, aye . . . but money to burn at a shop – never.

> In our house you didnae get anything you didnae actu'lly *need*. And sure you didnae need dollies. In our day 'needin' meant soup and tatties, or your boots gettin' sorted.

Few children, though, went quite without something to cuddle. They didn't have much in the Edgar home but Nellie remembers her dolls.

> I don't mind of havin' toys at all . . . except our cloth dolls of course . . . not bought mind, but because Faither worked in the calico print works and they printed doll-faces there. He used to bring home wee torn-off bits for dusters or sweat rags and my mother washed them and sorted out the bits wi' faces and sewed them up into dollies for us. Oh aye, we'd always our cloth dolls.

Boys cuddled their teddies when they were small of course, but the men remembering now recall better their skeely ways with diabolo or yo-yo. Diabolo ruled okay until the 1920s, but from then forward the yo-yo was the thing.

> You could do a lot of funny wee tricks wi' your yo-yo. Just plain 'upsy-down' was easy, or 'out 'n' in' and 'ower yer heidie' or 'cradley'. But the best was 'get along little doggie' when you kind of spun the yo-yo at the end of the string and walked it along the floor. Well I couldnae right enough, but Jimmy Gilchrist could. He could do them all.

If you were really stuck for something to do in the house when it was raining outside, there was always something at hand for inventing games.

> My granny had a sore back and there was a table-leaf kep' under the mattress on her kitchen bed. It was polished and shiny and when she was out we used to prop it from the bed and jam it against the fender. You got a rare slide down that.

Others raided the hall-stand and drawers.

> We'd a big lobby in our house and we used to get walking sticks and rolled-up socks to play a kind of hockey between the front door and the lobby press.

Board and chance games seem almost as old as memory.

> I play Ludo and Snakes 'n' Ladders wi' my grandweans and I mind playin' them wi' my granny, and I wouldnae wonder but she played them wi' hers. That would be what . . . seven generations? Fancy that!

But then, when you visit the Border abbeys they'll show you a scratched slab where, they say, King David I's abbey builders of eight centuries ago played their games of chance. So stakes on the throw of a dice are not new.

Nothing is . . . under the sun. Mary Hardy, at eighty-four, looks round at today's bairns building with Lego, cutting up their grubby pastry and heeshie-bawing their dolls.

> Oh aye, I see the weans doin' their jumpin'-ropes funny, and playin' wi' clever dollies that greet and wet their hippin's . . . but they're really no' doin' anything much different from what we were doin' in the 1900s or my own lassies in the 1930s . . . [She pauses . . .] I'm no' sure about them computers all the same.

20

I GOT ECCLEFECHAN RIGHT

Schools in Glasgow of the past century have come in all shapes, sizes and materials, from large ancient stone-built academies with centuries of tradition behind them, to the modern comprehensives sprawling over landscaped campuses. Between these two, in both type and period, there have been a variety of others. In the biener urban districts, with their tree-lined avenues, there were the little seminaries for young ladies, carried on mostly in gardened private villas. Then, each area of the inner-city had its board school which set out, late last century, to give a decent grounding to the tribes of children from teeming tenements, and to riddle out the lads and lasses o' pairts clearly destined for higher things. In the suburbs too, fast creeping out round the city in the inter-war years, authorities hastily threw up temporary wooden or corrugated schoolrooms to accommodate the new breed of semi-detached weans there. But whatever the style of the alma mater, all of them have been rich in plain talent and personality, and with teachers remembered with pain, pleasure and hindsight amusement.

There were all sorts of reasons for choice of school in the days before it was simply the local place or else pay fees at an old-established town grammar school. Mr Alexander Murdoch knows why he went to Bridgeton Secondary in 1898.

> The reason I went there from the old dominie at Tollcross, with his white beard and big red face was that, as a nipper my father kept rabbits with a boy called Robert Paterson, in a back-court at Greenhead

Street, and now that same Robert Paterson was heidie at Bridgeton Secondary. Mind he'd a lot of respect for Paterson forbye the rabbits, and thought any school wi' him in charge had to be good.

That school was a substantial building with real classrooms and echoing corridors, purpose-built in its time. Mrs Tait's early lessons, on the contrary, were in make-do and certainly cosier premises, but with an equally memorable teacher.

> Our school was just the room of a house really, and I had a tiny bird of a teacher there. She was a bloodless-looking wee thing but she was a rare teacher, and a stickler for good writing. D'you remember Vere Foster copy books? Well she was a great one for them, with their proverbs in joined-up writing along the top of each page and maybe five blank lines below to make better and better copies of it. I loved my Vere Fosters and got to be quite good at them . . . and quick . . . because when you were finished your page you got making toast at the schoolroom fire. But it wasn't just the writing she dinned in, it was other lessons and when I left her after a few years and went to a big academy I was well up with the others there.

And well enough grounded for a good classics degree by the end of the First World War . . . happily married too to the only heidie who ever palmied the compiler of this book.

> Out in the budding suburbs, by the turn of the century, houses were built before schools, and lessons took place in any suitable accommodation.

> There was no proper school our way when I was wee about 1904, but the classes were held in the two small rooms up the Orchardhill church tower, square rooms they were, with a coal fire in each and rare views across the hills round Glasgow. You went up the windy stair to the two teachers . . . Miss Johnson was one . . . but I can't just think on the other. Then, after that, the Tin Academy was put up nearer the main road and we all went down there with Miss Johnson. You stayed there till you sat your qually.

Apart from the fact that there were no fees, going locally to school had other homely advantages, and Miss Nan Gardner has a vision of one of those that would bring joy to the heart of an observant advertiser,

I was a bit lost and tearful when I went to school at first, so every morning at playtime my mother came to the school railings and passed a chocolate Vienna biscuit through to me. After sixty years I never see a chocolate Vienna but I think of my mother at that railing.

But there were perks in being at the posh schools too. With travelling money to manage, you could practise economies that were surprising in view of the substantial fees willingly handed over by your father. But perhaps it was just that the seeds of thrift and business acumen were being sowed.

I was at Glasgow Academy in the 1930s and I remember I used to walk from Kelvinbridge to the town to save the penny tram fare and get it to spend.

Some schools had airy assembly halls with elegant arches, pillars topped by classical mouldings and dux medallists listed in gold leaf. Some had little more of a hall than a tiled central corridor. Yet others had dunny-halls in deep wells below several storeys and surrounded by open stairways. In these last, some musician-teacher would start morning and afternoon school by thumping out marching music on the school piano while the 'lines' clumped upstairs to the classrooms and the janny prepared to take his first lot for drill in the hall. Classrooms, big or small, once reached, were much of a muchness everywhere, with blackboards, chalkdust, rows of desks in pairs, satchels at the feet and foreign bodies, various, stuffed down wally inkwells.

Just before we leave the architecture and fabric of schools to look at the memories of the pedagogy that went on inside, it's worth perhaps taking a glance at certain of its important precincts. And, as every schoolboy knows, whether the school was gracious and spacious, or simply your functional Corporation pile, it was sure to have notable lavvies for a variety of the kind of undouce shennanigans remembered by one dainty old lady after seventy-five years.

D'you mind when you were going to the toilets and you always asked your best friend of the moment to come and 'hold the door', just to stand outside holding it shut. You were maybe shy of the other girls but more likely the locks were broken and the boys threatened to lean over the top from their side to swing open the doors and look at you!

And the devil-may-care among the older pupils, boys and girls alike, indulged from time to time of course in the playtime 'puff'.

What of the classroom itself?

Ask any liberal-minded modern what schools were like in the 1930s and he'll no doubt assure you in almost Dickensian terms that they were nasty, brutish and dull.

But ask anyone who was actually a victim of those days and you get surprising answers. Of our rememberers certainly, not a single one but had mainly happy memories of schools and teachers. Such bad days as there were, were wryly recalled it's true, but only as black spots in otherwise interesting and purposeful years. Sure they stood in lines, did multiplication tables and regimented exercises to the teacher's counting, sat in rows, had Friday tests, gold stars and cleaning the board for good work . . . palmies for bad . . . (and not one but laughed at the word 'beating' used modernly for what they knew, and accepted with only small griping, as 'the belt'). The psychology may have been all wrong, but the educational errors of those old days are on the whole remembered philosophically. And recollections explode the myth that heads were constantly held down over sums and spellings and loathsome reading books, from nine till four without diversion.

> I mind of havin' wee honey-comb frame-things in a square box, maybe the size of a half-a-pound chocolates, and you got tiny coloured cubes, red and yellow, green and blue, white and black, and you put them into the wee spaces. You used it for counting and when you'd done your sums, you got making designs wi' the cubes.

That was around 1929 and from two or three years earlier there are those who remember knitting and plasticine, and an even more splendidly messy craft . . .

> You used to get treats on Friday afternoons after the register. I mind of takin' old newspapers to soak for makin' paper-mashy bowls and things. Then you painted them, put on a wee scrap and varnished over that.

They made doyleys and raffia bags for mothers' Christmases, compiled drawing books with works of crayon art; and Keating-copied Old Masters. In season they grew cabbages at the back of the school and bought them for a few coppers to take home. They rehearsed concerts, held Cake 'n' Candies for the 'poor' and organised bulb-growing competitions. Sometimes the ploys were approved curriculum, sometimes simply the whims of inspired teachers.

> We had a schoolmaster called David Horne. He'd been in the Army and he was a rigid stickler for discipline. But he was fair right enough, and we liked him. He'd a way of getting a notion suddenly and on a nice day he used to just stop the work suddenly and take the whole class off to Sir John Maxwell's estate at Pollok, right across the road from the school. He showed us all the different plants and trees and birds . . . even squirrels. And I once saw a beautiful kingfisher there.

Another who remembers a remarkable nature 'lesson', this time on the way back to school after lunch, was the lady who was once young Janet Macleod. Her home was just outside the city.

> I was with my brother going along a road with drystane dyking each side. He was playing his mouth-organ and we'd just passed a stretch of dyke when I happened to look back and saw . . . like a grey wave . . . a mass of weasels, as if they were rising and falling like sea, but on the road. We'd heard from the teacher about flitting of weasels, and we thought this was it. But Father said 'no', it was the sound of the mouth-organ that brought them out the wall.

Apart from handwork and wildlife outings there were other welcome breaks from lessons, even before the days of school milk.

We got wee mugs of Horlicks every mornin' at our school for a ha'penny. I liked it when it was my turn to go for the rack wi' the mugs in it. Then you got to collect the ha'pennies and take them back wi' the empties to the Horlicks lady.

There seem to be few embittered memories or twisted personalities among the rememberers, left over from these days of unsound teaching practice, when pupils expressing themselves uninvited, merited a passing clout; but even the rosiest blinkers cannot deny injustice or shame, and there's a punishment or two that still rankles after sixty . . . seventy . . . even eighty years.

I got the belt at school for writing a letter in the class to a boy called Peter Johnson. I don't know why ever to him because I didn't even like him. Another time I had to stand under the hall clock for talking in the line. That was worse than the strap because the heidie might see you and ask what you'd done.

I never smoked in the school sheds like some, nor nothing like that . . . but I mind of gettin' into trouble once. I was in a home and all the others in my class were just in their own families wi' mothers and fathers. They'd gardens too, and they brought flowers to the teacher. So when I saw that, I pinched some from a garden on my way to school. I got caught and didnae get to the qually party. The teacher offered to pay my ticket but the heidie wouldnae let her.

The Mr Harry Anderson of 1984 doesn't seem like one who would ever have threatened the peace of Albert Road Academy, but . . .

I once got the belt for pretending to fight with my desk neighbour . . . maybe a wee bit of horse play. But anyway the headmaster looked over the partition and saw us. He kept us sitting in his room for about two hours and then walloped us. He was a big tumphie really, him with his tile hat and frock-coat and dangling his gold watch chain.

Nor does Mrs Janet Purvis seem a natural villain, self-confessed prim wee teacher's-helper that she was, at Lochfield school in the early century.

I was put to the bottom of the class for talking to my friend about the Alvin Sawyer entertainers I'd seen on my holidays at Largs. Oh the shame of that . . . *me* at the bottom of the class! But there was worse to come. The inspector. He began to ask spellings and I was the only one that got Ecclefechan right . . . *and* five more words. But I got served right when he asked what such a good speller was doing at the bottom of the class and the teacher said I'd misbehaved . . . I would've been better to keep 'Ecclefechan' to myself.

And that was school . . . from the days of slates and sponges, penny-plain and tuppence-coloured books, and of brief sulks over scoldings, to the dawn of present enlightenment and teacher-pupil harmony . . . both a far cry from the long yonder schooldays of Mr Tom Watson's grandfather in the 1850s.

He used to tell me that all his schooling, before he went to work at a printer's, was three months at a penny-school in a dark close off Argyle Street, a cold bare room with rough benches. Every Monday the 'master' collected their pennies and went off with them to get drunk . . . just left the boys to do as they pleased. He learned nothing there, my grandpa, and when he left at nine years old, to work at feeding paper into a ruling machine, he couldn't write at all, and could just read but a word or two. He taught himself to read after that, from a book he got as a Bible prize, and to write from bits of the copy books they printed at his work.

Marching to music and the chanting of tables and lists of towns and dates with perjinkety teachers do not seem like gross hardships to thole in the face of that dour fight for education.

CADGERS AND HURLIE-MEN

They'll chuckle with mirth for sure in sixty years, at the memory of each other's wee round yirdfast bottoms in blue jeans, that they were ever the height of youthful fashion. They'll organise nostalgic societies to sigh over cars that crawl along at 80 m.p.h. with exhausts that puff out smoke, and they'll protest at the pulling down of quaint old concrete-and-glass office towers.

But look at your average stirring street of long since, and of now, and you can be certain that, if humanity has not destroyed itself, the same three elements will make up the city streets of the future, give or take trace-horse boy or traffic warden; penny-farthing or Fiesta hatchback; multi-block or jenny a'thing.

Streets are people, wheels and buildings, whatever their appearance and purpose.

Ordinary people, adults and weans, doing ordinary things, walk and dance through other pages in this book; the peever-ers and moshie-boys, kirk-goers and soldiers, shawlie-women and nurse-maids, hearse-followers and royal visitors. But they have all been bound for the places where they really belong, the rooms 'n' kitchens, the pews, the trenches, the grave. Those who belong to street-scenes may have lives apart, beds where they sleep, firesides where they sit, but for rememberers their place was the street, policemen and penny-jo's, buskers and hawkers and, perhaps most popular of them all, the lamplighters.

I mind the leeries lightin' the street lamps. They carried wee cutty ladders to get up to clean the glass or change the mantles. D'you mind the pole wi' the light in it that never went out? And the tinkly click when the pole went up and poked the glass flap open, and then the pool of grey-green light that came down?

I mind skimmin' up the lamp-posts to swing on the cross-bar, then dreepin' doon and runnin' away when the polis came.

Flower-sellers, hawkers and beggars had their pitches and every morning down Jamaica, Union and Argyle Streets came files of billboard men setting out from agencies to advertise hairdressers, cut-price bargains, restaurants and hell-fire.

Like Punch and Judy they were, wi' their heads pokin' up between their boards.

These were unconscious entertainers in their way, but real street buskers and musicians were as much part of the evening in town as the hall turns you paid to see . . . and whatever their particular skill, masters, most of them, of pavement patter as well.

You'll no' mind of Old Malabar. I saw him when I was wee, and heard him at his bawdy stories and street chaff, but his real thing was that he used to throw up a heavy ball and catch it in a leather cup strapped to his forehead. Mind his nose was all over his face wi' the times he'd missed, but he was a great turn.

Some hall-entertainers let passers-by taste their talent on the street in the hope of luring them inside for a full performance.

My grandfather knew one like that, this Jimmy Taylor that was around last century. Seems he had a right good conceit of himself and once when the owners of two different halls each wanted him, he auctioned himself in the open market-place at St Enoch Square. A big-big crowd gathered and my grandpa watched him get knocked down by the auctioneer to the highest bidder, for a huge pay of a £100 for the week.

But most of the buskers were outdoor-only performers.

D'you mind the way we used to gawp at the buskers outside of the picture-halls in Argyle Street? There was yon wee Egyptian that put down his board and clapper-danced on it. That would be in the 1920s. Then there was an organ-grinder wi' a monkey . . . you must mind of him in Union Street.

. . . and the paper-tearer, the tin whistler, the one-man band, the juggler . . . and a dozen others. Nancy Wall remembers one striking city-centre figure of the 1930s and '40s.

. . . a right kenspeckle figure of a man that played the fiddle. He'd an interesting, worn sort of face and a shock of iron grey hair . . . used to play outside the Georgic tearoom. D'you mind the Georgic?

He is recalled by others too as having been more tangibly recorded than in mere memory.

We used to see a painting of yon violinist in the Art Galleries. It was a good portrait that.

But ask any group of over-seventies, who was the best-known Glasgow street character of the century, and they come out in unison with one name, 'The Clincher'. Mr Duncan White remembers him well.

The Clincher oh aye. A tall, tall man he was, in a lum-hat and frockcoat or tails. He got his nickname from puttin' out a news-sheet that was called *The Clincher*. It was aye gettin' at the town council and the officials . . . takin' them down a peg. I mind him standing outside of Lewis's selling his sheet.

Another memory sees him on the move.

I mind seeing The Clincher one Christmas when he walked back and forward between Glasgow Cross and Jamaica Street with a sprig of mistletoe on his tail-coat. To kiss the lassies, I suppose.

But whether he lifted the coat-tail overhead to bestow his cheepers, the memory couldn't tell.

Och, he was a thorn in the breeks to a lot of folk was The Clincher, and there was once he got taken away to one of the asylums. Well, he was no more daft than the next chap and they had to let him out.

But he wouldnae go, not without a certificate that he was right in the head, and after that he used to say that he was the only sane man in Glasgow wi' a certificate to prove it.

Before the First World War such characters had their beats or pitches in the city centre, and the rest of pedestrian Glasgow, including wandering tykes and moggies, wove its way round and past them, jay-walking in its own whichever way. So too did much of the traffic. The earliest living memories of traffic are of carts, bicycles and cabs and, since many homes were still in the town, horse-drawn vans delivering milk, fish and bread. Wheels rumbled on the cobbles, steam-flanked horses snorted, and tossed great curls of mane and tail. Public transport added to the general stir and young Alick Murdock caught the end of one era.

I just remember the last of the horse-buses. They ran for about two years after I started to go into the town to school about 1897. They were three-horse buses that were stabled at Spittal's yard in Tollcross. I mind gangs of wee boys went after the horses with buckets and shovels to collect the manure to sell to folks with gardens.

And a very few years later, about 1900 horses that had pulled the old horse-trams were also finally put out to grass. By 1902 electric trams were on the go.

The trams were the same both ends. They'd outside stairs that curved up to open tops, where you sat wi' your gamp up when it rained.

Those trams provided interesting diversion for street-smart boys who seized adventure wherever it was carelessly offered.

You used to could go from one place to another on the trams for nothing. When you saw the conductor goin' away up the stair, you jumped on the running-board and got a hurl, hangin' on to the pole till he came down again. Then you got chased off that car and just waited for the next. Sometimes you were goin' somewhere, but mostly it was just for the ride. We used to hang on to the back of carts too and cadge a wee hurl from them.

Changes came in the design of trams over the years. They acquired roofs and upholstery and inside stairs.

They got to be quite comfy. I mind when we were young we used to take a pennyworth and go right to the terminus to see the driver swingin' back the overhead trolley and then changin' ends wi' the conductor. The driver used to close himself in wi' a gate-thing so's nob'dy could get on at his end. There was the bundy clocks too, where they stopped to get their time-cards punched.

For nearly forty years the real characteristic of the Glasgow tramcar was that the broad band of colour across the top half . . . green, red, blue or white . . . indicated its route direction . . . north, south, east, west. But in 1938, the new fleet of Coronation trams took to the rails, uniformly green and yellow, streamlined and modern. The 'red caurs' and the white or blue 'caurs' lingered on until they were worn out, but it was the end of an era and for the thirty-odd remaining years of its service the Glasgow tram was 'Coronation'.

The new cars looked quite nice but the older ones had wee compartments upstairs, front and back, and you used to get closed in there wi' your friends comin' home from the school and giggle and talk boys . . . and if your added-up tram ticket number could be divid' by seven, then the boy you fancied, fancied you!

It was fortunate that at least the trams ran in their appointed channels, for any old Glasgow street photograph tells that precious little of the other traffic kept strictly to lane. Cadgers and hurlie-men took their own short-cuts and weavings, and a one-time buyer in Macdonalds of Buchanan Street remembers them from the 1920s.

The suppliers used to send travellers with samples for buyers to look at. They'd come by train to Queen Street station and there was a rank of barrow men lined up there waiting on the train coming in. The travellers used to hire them to hurl their samples round the various stores.

One of the travellers too recalls the hazards of that.

The hurlie-men jouked in and out the traffic and you'd a rare old time of it keeping them in sight. We'd a lot of moneysworth in them barras. So you'd to watch out.

Trace-boys in West Nile Street, working up until the Second World War, also caused a fair bit of congestion although, when they did set out with a load, they led the horses in between two smooth hollowed tracks, for the easy rolling of cart-wheels.

The trace-lads used to sit in shop doorways watching their horses at the kerb and waiting for single-horse carts that were too heavy-laden to take the hill. Then they hired out their horses to haul them up the tracks. When I was wee I used to watch the Clydesdale horses feeding from their nose-bags and the pigeons all flutterin' around yon big shaggy feet to peck up the corn that fell on the ground. Oh aye, and when the horses moved off you used to could see sparks where their shoes struck against the cobbles.

D'you mind when they tried havin' wooden cobbles up the top of Buchanan Street, and then the rubber ones?

Cabs and carriages wheeled and changed course with little heed to other traffic and while their high-sitting drivers may have had a clear enough overall sight of the street, those at a lower level had their view dangerously blocked, and there are those who will tell you that it was no light undertaking to cross Argyle Street in the early century. But carriages remain in most memories as characteristic of a more gracious, or perhaps haughtier, age.

When I left school at fourteen in 1912 I went to work at Laing and Prentice, the ladies' outfitters in Sauchiehall Street. Next door was another very elegant dress shop called Grieve's. I can remember, at that time, that ladies coming to be measured and fitted arrived in carriages and left their footmen outside to wait for them. The men often stood there kicking their heels for long enough until their ladies came sweeping out in long skirts and into the carriages, sometimes with never a word to the men.

No doubt such ladies were born into the carriage 'set' but one of Glasgow's richest and most admired sons certainly was not.

Thomas Lipton was a close friend of my grandfather from when they were boys. Grandpa used to tell me that it was Lipton's ambition to see his parents in their own carriage and pair. My grandfather went with him the day he met the old people off the train from the country and handed them up to the new carriage drawn by two beautiful grey horses. My grandpa said Lipton stood there with tears in his eyes watching the driver moving off with them in their grand new turn-out.

Buildings of the Glasgow at the turn of the twentieth century, apart from slums mercifully flattened, or fine blocks and churches less mercifully mown down by planners, are still there to be seen and enjoyed in their refurnished glory . . . the hotels, circuses, crescents, colleges, shops and well-ordered sweeps of tenements. And if the eye can blot out the more recent additions (and enjoy the best of them another time) Glasgow, as the rememberers knew it, is still there.

We've looked at tenements and churches in other chapters so let a few of the shops serve to give a glimpse of the buildings on the street scene. As well as those high-class establishments where carriages disgorged the clientele at Charing Cross, there were many other well-known names that made Sauchiehall Street, Buchanan Street and the rest, famous and fashionable in their heyday; and made one lady grue, at the query of a new-met Edinburgh acquaintance. 'D'you never come shopping to Edinburgh?' What! With Coplands, Gardners, Wyllie & Lochhead's at the end of a tram ride!

Sauchiehall Street was lovely. (Did you know that 'sauchs' are willows and that long ago the haughs of the Clyde were covered with willows, like the Broomielaw was with broom?) Anyway there were fine shops there when I was young. Copland & Lye, Treron, Daly's . . . all good expensive stuff . . . I'm talking of Colonel Daly's time mind. Then in Pettigrew and Stephen's you could sit at your tea and listen to the orchestra.

Those were the streets in the heart of the town, but there were more village-like aspects in the side-streets and on the outskirts.

In my earliest mindings of the streets round Ibrox in 1892 there was no cars yet, just a few gigs and pony-traps. The doctor had one and drove around his calls sitting up there in his lum hat and frock coat.

And he would have to steer his way among carts and barrows, scooters, girds, bicycles, old clo'es women and the ubiquitous Glasgow shawlies.

Och I mind my mother could pass a nice afternoon airing the wean in her shawl and meeting her friends for a chat . . . Now, what else was there in the street? . . . Oh aye, the Co-op coal-cart and d' you remember yon narrow carts they could back right in the butchers' doorways with whole carcases in them, so's they didnae have to carry them from the street? More the shape of coffins? Then there was the chap we called Late-and-Early, with his milk float, that you didnae know whether you were gettin' last night's milk late or the next day's early. And there was the soordook cairt wi' the buttermilk.

One who went out with the soor dook in another district was young Jimmy Wisner.

I was just a laddie then and I got to ride with the soor-dook man and shout for him.

'Soor dook, thruppence-a-jug, soor dook!'

No, we never took it over your way . . . too toffy-nosed there for soor dook.

He went on to greater things though, than promoting soor dook, for he grew up to have streets named after him for dedicated service to the community. Another lad who did a hawker's street cries for him, was Duncan White.

I went wi' the fishmonger's cart, and shouted, 'Tripe, best tripe . . . tripe-bags!'

Telling you that, it brings back the street to me, clear as clear, wi' the boys taking steppies on the carts till the carter chased them, and me delivering fresh and skim milk twice a day for two shillin'-a-week. Did I get keepin' it? Did I hang? Your mother was aye waiting on it when you got home.

All day long provision carts trundled the streets and then when it began to get dusky of a winter evening . . .

> The horse-vans used to have wee lights flickering front and back. I liked that for I kent our teas would be ready on the table.

The shops of these side-streets too were a little different from the Dalys' and Grieves' and the high-class Italian warehousemen of the town. Mrs Milree remembers the Queen's Park area.

> When I was wee the fishmongers used to have water running down their windows and we used to pretend to lick it as it came scooshing down, and feel the window cold on your tongue.

Few streets within a radius of six miles of Glasgow's centre were outwith earshot of a clanging tram trolley, but in the elite residential suburbs there were also grander versions of town carriages and Mrs Muriel Lillie remembers their stately progress along Nithsdale Road with an occasional interesting mishap.

> Sometimes on a frosty day when the cobbles were slippery, you used to see a horse stumble and go down. Then the men seemed to have to sit on the horse's head to calm it down and put a hood over its face to get it to its feet again.

But for that same young lady carriage travel was not only spectator-sport.

> My family used to hire a landau sometimes, to take my grandmother for a drive and I used to get to go with her. So, there was me in my wee best coat driving like a lady with my granny all round Maxwell Park. The landau had a hood that came up snug when it was wet or windy, and went down if it was sunshine.

Mr Harry Anderson, too, has a street memory of long-ago Pollokshields:

> When I was a wee lad about 1907, sometimes on Sundays when we came out of Albert Drive Church on to Darnley Street, we used to see four-horse charabancs coming along, full of bad people going on Sunday trips. These charas were very noisy and the horses set up clouds of dust with their hooves . . . no tarmac you see.

Although horse-traffic in haulage and delivery-service in city and suburb didn't entirely die out between the wars, the arrival of more lethal vehicles demanded new disciplines of lane, speed and signal. Street scenes became less of a circus and more of a purring progress towards destinations with only changes in the shape and colour of cars and vans to mark the years. The Second World War drew a final curtain over what was left of that cheerful wayward bustle in Glasgow streets. Black-out and austerity brought sudden change instead of the slow evolution they had known before . . . the neon elephant tossing his trunk above Pickard's cinema, the other lighted cartoon adverts, the great Capstan banner across the Hielan'man's Umbrella, all snuffed out. Almost the last of the horses (except those pulling the Black and White whiskey drays) turned finally into city stables before retirement. Hooded lamps, tramcars with painted windows and dim-blue lights inside, dun coloured vehicles, sandbagged buildings, made a dismal scene.

No doubt there will be nostalgia some day for what emerged of people, buildings and wheels, on the Glasgow street-scene after the war, even for the bleak demolishing years before graceful flyovers louped the wastelands and the stonework began to come up smiling again. But not yet.

DON'T CALL ME WONDERFUL

They say that death, not sex, is the taboo subject of our time. Is it? Is it not perhaps that not so many meet it intimately in their young lives and there seems no need to get het up about it until nearer the three-score and ten, or the time for sheltered housing? Of course there are tragedies that caw the feet from us and stop us in our tracks, but it's their very unthinkableness that stuns.

> You know fine death's comin', but it's no' so much part-parcel of your day-by-day life the way it was when we were young and there was a lot more killin' diseases. There's that much to think about just livin', you cannae forever be harpin' on about somethin' that's comin' anyway. Maybe it'll no' be that long right enough but you just try and live right and get ready wi' God . . . but no' to go out lookin' for death.

A patronising murmur to the 95-year-old philosopher that she's wonderful, brings a richly merited rebuke.

> Don't call me wonderful. I hate folk to say I'm wonderful. I'm just *here*.

Bereavement was certainly part and parcel of everyday life at all levels until around the mid-1940s. Apart from the grim casualty lists of both wars, all those who can recall their own experiences in the previous six decades and one or two handed-down tales from their elders paint vivid memory pictures of death and illness.

> My grandfather used to tell me that his grandmother and most of her generation were pock-marked, some of them so badly that a lot of bairns were feart to look at them. But among the older people it was just an accepted thing. He told me too about his mother

dying of cholera when he was about six in the 1850s. She'd had it before but this time he minded seeing her lying fighting for breath on the kitchen floor and his older brothers trying to rub away her dreadful cramps. That was the way the cholera took you. She died though, for all the rubbing.

There was an echo of death too in this eerie tale of a grandfather from the 1870s.

My grandpa told me that he was once sent by his catering employer to look over the old Wellington Church in Waterloo Street to see if it would do for function premises. It was a Saturday afternoon and he was alone in the basement when the wind slammed the door shut. His candle snuffed out too and he fell into a kind of big long hole. When he got used to the near dark he found he'd tumbled into one of the graves in the old kirk crypt and there were all these other ones round him as well.

There was no explanation of how Grandpa was rescued from this gloomy predicament but he certainly didn't moulder there for ever, because the place did become the Waterloo Rooms for functions, when the bodies had been moved to the Glasgow Necropolis to lie peacefully beside John Knox and Wee Willie Winkie.

There are grim memories too of the fate of the flotsam souls of Glasgow's archways and dunnies, whose cravings denied them even the meanest comfort at the end of their days. Drink and drugs still take their toll but there can't be many living now who ever saw the 'drunk barras' of the city. Mr Tom Watson's father told him about those.

The police would go round at night with a flat barrow, picking up drunks from pavements or gutters, then tip them out somewhere more sheltered, to sleep off their dwam. Then, come the morning, the barras went round again to gather up the ones that hadn't survived the night and take them to the morgue.

Recollections of illness and death after that are within living memory. In 1901 there was a serious outbreak of smallpox and, on 5 April of that year, eleven new cases were admitted to Belvidere Hospital to join the 250 already taken in during the epidemic.

That was more than eighty years ago, but the legacy lingers in more than that statistic of long ago.

> There was this big-big outbreak of the smallpox in the year the old queen died. Two weans in my class took it and everyone got innoculated. My friend's wee sister, Lucy, was just a baby at the time but she got done and she come deaf and a wee bit coofy after that and she's been like that all her days since.

Fevers were a scourge of past days too. Mrs Mary Milree still shudders at the memory of the Fever Van.

> Scarlet fever and typhoid and the measles were very very common and you got the colly-wobbles when you saw the van coming down your street to take away whoever had the fever to Belvidere Hospital. It was all hush-hush and mysterious because the van windows were smokey blue and you couldn't see through. If scarlet or typhoid or even the measles was in your house you were kept off the school for so many weeks till the infection was gone. They burned your school books as well. Everyone dreaded those fevers and the diphtheria too of course.

Very occasionally a milder case was nursed at home and some-times one disease was complicated by another.

> When we lived in a tenement it was a bottom flat wi' no bathroom and just the outside toilet. But we didnae share it wi' anyone. Just as well, for when one of my girls had the 'dip' there was scarlet going as well and the doctor said we were lucky that no one else used the toilet or my lassie would've got the fever along wi' the diphtheria and there was no sayin' . . .

and decades later, Mrs Margaret Henderson still shakes her head over that unfinished sentence.

If the victim was left at home there were strict rules of sanitation.

> Your ma had to put up a blanket over the room door, wrung-out of disafectan', and then after that the fumigatin' man came and burned sulphur or some-such on a shovel to make the place safe again. Mostly folk got over whatever it was and came back to school, but they were often gey peely-wally an' wi' their hair cut off. But

sometimes they died and then you stood behind your curtain and watched their funeral, feart that it could easy be you, next time.

There were other hazards too before a youngster could properly be claimed to have survived childhood and be ready to face the risk of teenage tuberculosis.

My mother lost two babies at different times from the whooping-cough, both of them called William. When a third boy arrived she couldn't bring herself to have another William. So he was John.

Another wheezy crickle that sounded alarm bells was the croup.

In our family there was me and my half-sisters Betty and Frances. I mind when Betty had the croup. They boiled up kettles of water for the steam to break the croup and try to get her breathin' again, for she was just gaspin'. I can see her yet. She was a right bonnie wean wi' black curls and rosy cheeks. But she died of that croup.

The funeral of a child taken away in its small white kist was, and is, heart-rending, but any funeral in olden days was more sombre and spectacular than today's stream of limousines purring swiftly and silently among the rest of the traffic to the crematorium.

I mind of the big Clydesdales wi' the black plumes and gear, that used to rumble the funeral carriages over the cobbles to the graveyard, when I was young.

A more personal tragedy and the funeral after it has lived a long time in Mrs Rose Lindsay's memory of the early 1920s.

My mother had nice long hair that was piled up and I used to like to stand on a wee stool and take the hair-pins out, so's it fell all round her shoulders. Well, this night, I can just see mysel' doin' that. It was Hogmanay. My mother said she smelled smoke and right enough the house down the stair was on fire. My father couldnae get the door open for to get down so he opened the window, threw down a rope and told us to get out. My sister went first, then me, the both of us dropped safe-enough into a blanket. But at my mother's turn, a corner of the blanket was let go and she fell and hit her head. She was expectin' too and she had the baby right enough but she was never hersel' after, and a wee while later, when she was ill in her bed, I mind her sayin' . . . 'It's awfu' cold, come in beside me Rose, girl.' So I went in under the clo'es and she just died there beside me. I was about twelve.

And the picture of the funeral three days later is still etched in the memory.

> I mind when she was to be buried, the big black horses standin' outside, frothin' at the mouth, and me just standin' there at the close watchin' them takin' my wee mother away in a black coffin. It was horrible.

Girlhood snapped shut for Rose Lindsay that day. She didn't go to the graveside. That part of the proceedings belonged to the menfolk at any funeral. Even small boys were not exempt. Most of them walked in their first procession at the burying of a grandparent.

> When my grandpa died I was comin' up twelve, and me and my wee brothers (they would be maybe ten and seven), we a' wore wee dark suits and bowler hats to walk to the graveyard. It was all walkin' funerals then.
>
> I was at my grandpa's funeral a long time before the First World War. It was a horse-drawn hearse and we followed it on from Camden Street to Caledonia Road. There was nothin' fancy about it, nothin' dressed-up. We'd just black ties like, and wee bowlers. It was only the men and boys followed the coffin, the women just stayed at home and got ready the steak pie. Mind I don't think we'd steak pie that day . . . too dear . . . just be a cup of tea and maybe bridies.

There's not a lot of light relief in clash about death and funerals, but if a child wasn't taken up personally with a death and lived near a funeral undertaker there was endless interest and drama to be had from strangers' funerals.

> We stayed near the undertaker's in Pollokshaws. He was a very popular undertaker . . . easy the best for funerals around that part of Glasgow . . .

and the innocent query to that rememberer, 'Was it Wyllie and Lochhead's?' she laughs at your folly.

> Och dearie me, no! Wyllie and Lochhead's was for when you died in Newlands . . . no' Pollokshaws!

Long after the parlour blinds were up again, the clock restarted from the time of death and the funeral flowers withered, there were other continuing death rituals in the early days of the 1900s.

> I don't know about other places, but round us when a woman died in childbed leavin' her baby, the wee soul had bits of black ribbon in its bonnet and sometimes in its pram pillow!

and even after death at the other end of life . . .

> When I was six in 1905 my granny died and I got two black outfits at the dressmakers, one for the school and one for Sundays.

These conventions were still flourishing ten and more years later. Mrs Hilda Gibson remembers her father's death in 1915.

> I was eight and I was dressed in black from hair-bow to boots. My sister was seven years older and ready to leave school.
>
> I was all in black. It was quite the usual thing to have two or three in the class in mournings for some kin or other. I mind Mr Watson, my teacher at Queen's Park school, stopping me in the playground and asking quite kindly . . . I mind his very words, 'Dear me, Dorothy, and who have you been losing?'

The return to ordinary clothes was in stages.

> Near the end of mourning-time for Papa I went to a party in a white broderie-anglaise dress wi' black ribbons threaded through it and black trims.

Smallpox, measles, typhoid, TB, and by the late teens of the century there was a new toll. There had always been accidents with wheel and horse, but now there were fast-moving cars, and in the early days weans were not so schooled in traffic-codes as they are now, bunnets and school-bags carried no rhymes or fluorescent bands and lollipop persons were unknown.

> I mind my cousin's wean dyin'. He was just a toddler and here he dropped his dummy-teat on the edge of the street. He leaned over to get it and a motor car came by and struck him. Killed him. There was a wake for that wee chap.

Wakes could be roistering affairs, enjoyed in the earnest notion that it was doing old Tom or Joe an honour and giving him the very kind of send-off he would have favoured and savoured himself . . . just the way he would have wanted it . . . a pious certainty many have, of the wishes of dead friends . . .

> Many's the wake I've been to, oh aye. A wake's just sittin' up a' night, in the same room's the coffin. Some call it a lich-wake and it's just keepin' the dead company between the dyin' and the bur-yin'. You say the rosary and sometimes you play cards and drink tea . . . aye and stronger than tea, forbye. It's all to keep you from goin' to sleep. A right wake can sometimes get a wee bit out-hand . . . but that wee thing's wake wasnae like that, poor bairn.
>
> I mind the wee white coffin open in the middle of the room and the tiny waxy boy lyin' in it wi' his baby hands claspin' on a bunch of snowdrops. There were candles all round and everyone sayin' the rosary at the right times through the night. I've aye had that sad wee white picture in my mind.

There's scarcely a one born before 1910 or so, talking of young days, who doesn't speak of the flu epidemic that ravaged Europe just after the Armistice of 1918 and of friends who died in it. Men and women who had survived the most fearful war in his-tory, even some who were still in military hospitals recovering from wounds, fell to the killer flu.

> I was nursing in a military hospital when the big flu came. Pa-tients and nurses died like flies and the staff nurses' home had to be turned into a ward. A lot of the girls died as well as the men, and some of them that did survive were left wi' things like sleepy-sickness and fits. It was a wicked flu that.

But healthier days were coming, and year by year the fevers and the rickets, the smits of single-end and shared cludgy, and the risks of childbirth dwindled as medical skills and health care increased.

> I taught in Glasgow schools for forty years and the change in the health of children was astonishing over the years. The evacuation

alerted folk to a lot of hardship and lack of care among the weans. Afterwards teachers watched for everything, and sent every rash, sniffle and itch to the school clinic. Eyes, teeth, feet and heads were examined and all sorts of things were nipped in the bud.

That was Miss Isobel Cameron's experience between the 1920s and the '70s, and a fellow-teacher bears her out.

It was a lot more work for the schools, mind you, but I never yet met a teacher that objected to Teenie having her jags or what d'you McCallum getting his verrucas seen to.

A teacher of more recent years adds her observations.

In my mother's day there were families in her school raddled with TB so that maybe two or three in the same house died or were years in hospital. I started teaching in 1947 and I never once in thirty years had a child in a class that died of TB or any of the fevers . . . a few cancers, aye, and accidents, but the other things, no. And not many children had to face the death of parents.

So maybe it's not surprising that people, meeting less frequently with untimely death, don't talk so often about it, or brood so much on the prospect, as bairns who had the chitters every time they saw the Fever Van or heard that a classmate had the 'dip'.

MEDALS DINNAE COMPENSATE

In many a douce wee sitting room in Glasgow, the kind called 'little boxes', by foolish folk who judge that rows of like houses contain rows of like minds and life experience, there are mementoes and echoes of wartime adventure, tragedy, humour and endurance which along with life's other pummellings and small triumphs, make ordinary people into uniquely moulded, one-off individuals.

We've already captured a few of the memories of the First World War which erupted into such a stark and bitter shock to those who had waved their flags at the beginning. The Second World War came to more reluctant but better-prepared people who had watched its approach with dread, not bunting.

> Hitler was a kind of brooding monster, a dark shadow out there when I was wee. I was feart for him for all the things my faither said. He used to say he wouldnae trust that man an inch and he didnae like him comin' to be the leader in Germany.

> When we began to see the war gettin' closer all I could think on was my own time in the trenches and the green kind of mist that was the poison gas of 1915 comin' across No Man's Land. And now I had three grown sons that were the age for soldiers.

There were plenty of signs of the coming war, fed by tales from European holiday-makers in the 1930s, and by word of the kind of brief adventure had by John Kent, a young Glasgow minister in the summer of 1939. His wife tells of the incident.

> John always travelled on the continent during his month's holiday and that particular year he had been asked by the Armenian mission

in this country to collect money belonging to the mission, that was lying in a German bank. It was August and his contact was a man called Minker.

They met. Minker was friendly and warned him not even to try to get the money because the authorities would never let it go, but to get himself out the country as fast as possible. John was travelling by car and this Minker offered to come and guide him towards the border. He hid in the back of the car and while they were driving down the road they passed swarms of German troops doing some exercise or other. At a bend when the road was clear Minker shouted to John to drive fast to the border and he jumped out of the car himself and scrambled down a bank into the cover of trees. John was only across the border two or three days, when the Germans marched down that same road into Poland.

On 3 September, war came.

I mind of that day like it was last week. We were at the kirk and the beadle came in and handed up a note to the pulpit, and the minister read out what Chamberlain had said on the wireless. We'd just a short service that day and I sat there terrified, and sure that before we got home the bombs would be droppin', like in the newsreels about Spain and Abyssinia. They were nightmares to me these news pictures when I was wee.

To another child, of twelve, it was the end of a chapter.

That day was like a kind of terminus to my childhood because we'd three much younger cousins came evacuated to us from nearer the middle of the town. The maid had opted to be 'bombed' with her own family so now there were shoes to clean, dishes to wash and the wee cousins to look after. I was likely enough growing out of it but I don't mind of ever really playing, again.

If war is ever tidy this 1939 war was tidier than the 1914 one. Call-up was organised from the start, air-raid precautions ready, and evacuation planned. Glasgow prickled with Lord High Every-things in arm-bands, and conscripted servicemen quietly catching trains for initial training centres. No rush-muster or recruiting hullabaloo this time. Call-up lasted throughout the war and long after, but it always took the same form.

I remember the day Jim was called up. The postman rang the bell. 'There's your man's call-up papers. I've delivered that many I know them whenever I see them.'

Jim Lillie went to the Army. Joe Kyle went to the Navy.

I was called up at thirty-eight years old. I was a banker, married with a young baby and at first I went on to the lower deck of a destroyer and slept in a hammock. It was a big change, I can tell you, from the bank and the comfortable home in the suburbs.

The girls were in the call-up too this time. Janey Brown was one of them.

I was called to the Air-force . . . to the WAAF. You'd your bad times and your good but afterwards you forgot the weary miserable times and just minded the fun. I got stationed at Norfolk and was the whole war as a cook.

The home front was mobilised quite quickly too. In Glasgow the first big concern was to get young children away from the city centre to areas reckoned safe. The evacuation was planned in detail beforehand, but, even so, there was an inevitable stramash when the real thing came. Isobel Cameron was a teacher directed away with a batch of fearful city weans.

Our instructions were that if the war came we'd to gather at the school right away. It was a terrible feeling packing your bags for off, without knowing where you were going or when you'd be back. We felt like the trails of refugees you saw on the Pathescope news.

We'd no idea where we were bound until after the train left Parkhead Cross, and then we were told 'Perth'. What a journey! Hundreds of mothers, weans and bawling infants packed like herring, and no toilet on the train! Things were that dire by the time we got to Auchterarder we'd to get the train stopped. But just think on yon wee platform at Auchterarder with its one toilet and dozens of weans dancing desperate on that train. What could you do?

'Everybody out! Boys . . . all go and perform down that side of the train. Girls . . . come on now . . . down the other side!'

Then back to the train for the last lap.

At Perth we were herded into the ice-rink all labelled. It was like a slave market, us all lined up in rows and a wee man with a bellowing voice and two lists in his hand, one of hosts and one of Glasgow children. Oh what an uproar of greetin' and girnin' from frightened tired weans, away from home . . . maybe forever for all they knew!

One of the evacuating mothers who went in the opposite direction was Helen Stewart.

I was to be evacuated with my girls and we'd to meet at the school on the Sunday morning, the minute the news came over the wireless if it was war. So there was me, leavin' my man behind, and standin' wi' my three wee lassies in their covert coats wi' labels tied to their button-holes and makin' sure my money was safe.

'You just sew a wee pooch into your stays, Nellie,' my mother had insisted. She thought nothing could go amiss if I'd that wee pocket in my stays. It was midnight when we got the length of Dumfries and I was wabbit and near weepin'. The billeting man put us in a nice enough house, but along with other Glasgow folk that I thought were that rough and coarse.

It was my fault, I was too upset to give them a right chance, for they would be good-hearted people just as upset as I was. I made up my mind to come home, although the officers tried to persuade me to stay. But I was thrawn and next day I trailed my wee lassies all back to Glasgow, and we just plowtered on through the war at home after that.

Within a few weeks, people settled into the first phase of wartime routine with very few folk, over the age of twelve, playing no part at all in the war effort.

I was an air-raid warden round our way. You went about checking stirrup-pumps and buckets of sand and water. That was alright, but you didnae half get cold shoulder when you went to a door to tell them there was a chink of light showing through their curtains in the blackout. I often think on Dave Willis and his 'air-raid warden' song:

In my wee gas mask I'm workin' out a plan.
Tho' all the kids imagine that I'm just a bogey man
The girls all smile, and bring their friends to see
The nicest-lookin' warden in the ARP.
Whenever there's a raid on, listen to my cry
'An airy-plane, an airy-plane away-way-up-a-kye.

> Then I run helter-skelter, but don't run after me
> You'll no' get in my shelter for it's *far too wee.*

Mrs Jean Tait remembers her war work as being a model of preparation for disaster.

> I was attached to the first-aid post. Doctor Anderson gave us a good grounding in emergency treatment and we all had shifts, so the post was manned day and night.

Others maintained a constant after-dark vigil . . . with companions.

> My father was a squaddie fire-watcher, and funny enough he worked with three Browns in his roster. There was Aluminium Brown who was in that line of business, Salmon Brown that was a rare angler, and Poison Brown the pharmacist. They watched out for even wee fires that could help the German bombers. D'you mind the slogan 'Fires help Hitler'? That was on a lot of posters. So was 'Careless Talk Costs Lives', that was for fear of spies.

For many years it had been traditional for country folk and travelling people to harvest the acres of soft fruit in Perthshire, but many of them were called up or placed in essential work, and so it fell to school children to do the berry-picking.

> We went every summer for about four years to the berry-picking at Blairgowrie. We got paid a penny a pound for rasps, and some got quite quick at it, but not like some of the tinks that were the real pickers. They could fill two or three luggies for every one of ours. They were interesting people and they used to sing and play fiddle music in the bothy-place at night.

Glasgow won a good name among British cities for its service to troops passing through or stationed nearby.

> I worked in two different canteens. We did four-hour stints and maybe three shifts a week. There was the YMCA in Buchanan Street and the churches' canteen. It was heavy work when maybe a troop train came in with droves of hungry men and women. There were other canteens all over the city too.

Mr William Stevenson, as stalwart a citizen in this war as he had been soldier in the First, used his building expertise in his voluntary service.

I was leader of a wee emergency team set up to go digging or shifting rubble if there was bombing and for a long while it looked as if we wouldnae ever be needed, but we were, later.

Elderly ladies had work groups to make oiled-wool sea-boot stockings, hospital slippers, or balaclavas for search-light units . . . even for Home Guards.

I was in the Home Guard . . . Was it like *Dad's Army*? . . . no, no, it was better 'n *Dad's Army*. It's true enough we drilled wi' broom handles at first, but we really trained quite well and did our watching up at Corkerhill. We'd some right pompous wee officers right enough, that didnae know much about drill, and I mind going up early one night and here's two of them sittin' hearkenin' each other out the wee drill book.

And there was nursing.

I did voluntary nursing at the Royal Infirmary when they were short, and had a lot of valuable experience for the time when the bombing came.

The air-raid precaution work, the canteens, the first aid, the Home Guard and even the little knitting and sewing work-parties, were all voluntary activities, but other people were directed into work vacancies left by the young called up to the services.

I was made to be a clippie in the war. If you werenae in the Forces you got sent to what they called essential work, munitions or that. Wi' me it was the buses. It was quite cold in the winter and it was difficult at night in the black-out because you'd only a kind of dim blue light inside the bus for takin' fares and countin' your change.

Some found new purpose in their own daily work and even a perfectly legitimate by-product boost to business.

By 1939 I ran a wee cobbler's business alongside my joinery and when the Rouken Glen was turned to a big, big Army camp with trucks and lorries and thousands of troops I got the job of doing their shoe and boot repairs.

School teaching too widened in variety and challenge in some respects, and narrowed itself down to essentials in others.

I was teaching in Bridgeton and the Fire Service took over the bottom floor of the school. Classes were on shifts and you'd fifty to teach in the mornings and fifty in the afternoons. There was just time for the three Rs and no frills. After one bombing when the upstairs was damaged I taught for long enough downstairs with the weans sitting on mattresses among stirrup-pumps. When the radiators got hot the smell of heated rubber was suffocating. I used to think to myself. 'Oh my, imagine that perished rubber going out to a fire sometime.'

Alongside all these public preparations and precautions against bombing and invasion these were the pinpricks and vexations of daily wartime life . . . remembering to carry gas masks, coping with ration books, running with potato peelings and leftovers to the neighbourhood swill bin, sticking unsightly anti-splinter netting on window panes for fear of air raids. But that was all small thole while young men and women were facing the waste of real war.

My most vivid memory of the Navy wasn't a battle, it was a terrible storm when we were off the Irish coast at one stage. The sea was like grey walls heaving up and crashing down over you again and again. That day I was really afraid. Later we went minesweeping off Grimsby and we convoyed and escorted the big Mulberry harbours down the east coast.

That was Joe Kyle's memory, and here is Elizabeth Dewar's of her father . . .

My father was involved in the famous *Laconia* incident, when the survivors in the lifeboats were taken in tow by the German U-boat which had sunk the ship. But it had to cut them adrift and crash dive when it was bombed itself by an American aircraft from the Azores. The survivors were left hundreds of miles from the West African coast, and a lot of them like my father died from exposure.

And there were those who operated from nearer home but just as dangerously.

Three of us, me and the two Jimmys, went to the RAF. We were just eighteen, all air crew. In June 1940 I got taken prisoner and I was five dreich years a prisoner. Then I came home, but the two Jimmys didnae.

Except for the sound and fury of ack-ack guns, signifying not very much, Glasgow itself was far behind the battle-lines, until 1941 brought the noise and smell and sight of actual war to Clydeside with the blitz. People opened their homes to bombed-out and bereaved victims.

> The day after the Greenock blitz we'd a young boy sent to us as an evacuee. He was in a real state of shock. He'd run up the hill behind Greenock when the bombing started, carrying his baby sister and lain over her all night to protect her with his body.

And Mr William Stevenson's little unit of tradesmen-rescuers, in business at last, was sent to Clydebank during the devastating air raids there. They found the main part of the town utterly destroyed and it was reckoned later that in three nights of bombing only twelve houses in the whole of Clydebank were undamaged. They dug out the dead and injured, with bombs still exploding around them.

> I mind one house that was just a heap of rubble except for a bit of stairway you could just see, away-way deep in. They thought there was someone trapped there, so says I, 'Cut out a coupla risers and treads and make a way in there.' Under all the sandstone and plaster and roofin' we found an old woman and a wee lad both sittin' on the stair, dead, the old body clutchin' on to a handbag wi' £400 in it.

Mrs Janet Purvis recalls her work during the same week at Clydebank.

> Thousands were bombed out their houses and ever so many people lying injured. But the queer funny wee thing that I remember so vividly was the sight of all the folks' budgies bombed out their cages and fluttering about in a frenzy . . . green and blue and yellow. It was bizarre really in all that devastation, and I can see those budgies yet. But the real job was to see to the injured and set up canteens to feed people in whatever bits of building were still standing until other arrangements were made for them.

Stray sticks of bombs landed too in areas in and around Glasgow that were patently not targets.

A lot of funny things happened the night our road got bombed. My uncle ran with his stirrup pump and bucket to put out a fire, but here he forgot to take water in his pail. He took a lot of snash afterwards from his friends for that.

And then next-door's greenhouse light flashed on by itself (maybe with the thudding of the bombs) and everyone was screaming for somebody to smash the lamp before the Germans saw our street and bombed us to pulp.

In the morning we'd a thirty-foot crater in our garden and six others in a line down into the next road. Even a clothes pole, with a big concrete blob on the bottom, had sailed over a roof from a back garden and landed on the road.

As they cleared away the debris and called in the emergency builders for makeshift repairs there was a lot of dark muttering over that maverick stick of bombs.

We blamed it all on our local spy. He was a Mr Brown that had worked in Germany before the war and had a German mistress living with him in our road. Everybody remembers how he'd thought Hitler was a great chap early on, and when he came back from wherever he'd been that night nob'dy spoke much to him for years, even though you knew fine that it couldnae be true that he'd had our wee suburb singled out for attacking. But mind, he shaved his head just like you saw Germans at the time.

Sense of humour creams up again though, when shock is past, and Mrs Margaret Kent recalls an incident after a raid which sent 300 people to be bedded down in their church hall emergency centre.

One man told me he was a baker and could I waken him at three o'clock in the morning to go and see the state of his bakery whether he could turn out his usual batches. I went to the hall with these rows and rows of sleeping people to waken him at three, and then realised I didn't know which of the 300 he was.

There was selfless and faithful work done in Glasgow during the six years of the war but the highlight and glory was reserved for one local farmer and his wife, the Eaglesham Dad's Army and the Giffnock police.

I was about fourteen and I was walking home in the black-out one night and you could hear a plane quite clear. Then the engine cut out. It was awful funny . . . suddenly just nothing and no airfield near. Next day all the rumours were fleein' about that there'd been a crash on the moor, a farmer'd taken in a German spy and got the Home Guard, and that now he was in our Scout hall or maybe the cell at the police station. Then the next far-fetched tale was that Rudolf Hess had landed somewhere in Scotland and it didnae take long for folk our way to put two and two together and guess that the rumours were about the same thing.

All the boys cycled out to the farm to see this crashed plane. My brother took home two wee bits of it for souvenirs; before he even knew it was Hess' right enough.

William Stevenson gives his account of that same strange incident.

Tom Hyslop, the police inspector, was a friend of mine and came to my house early hours one morning. 'There's a plane come down, up by, Willie. I want you to come wi' me and see it.'

And away we goes to where the crash-land was, at a farm field. They still didnae know then for sure who the pilot was. It was that hard to believe his claim that he was Hess. Anyway the Home Guards had taken him to the Giffnock jail. We went into the plane and Tom handed me a metal label that had got torn off in the crash. I have it here yet, that wee minding off of Hess' plane.

It's years now since Hess lost his aircraft and Willie Stevenson went out with his inspector friend to find it. Both surely remembered that night in their different ways. But the one filled half a lifetime since then, with other memories, and lived his latter years in the freedom and companionship of home, while the other, of much the same age, paced out his empty years in loneliness and captivity.

After the Clydeside blitz local people could feel more keenly for the battered folk of the south, but its own worst days were over. War work went on, belts were tightened yet again, and then at last it was finished.

I mind the Armistice in 1918 and the kind of two-stage one in 1945, and they were quite different. It was quieter in 1945. Nobody went mad the way they did before.

Perhaps that was because the euphoria of 1918 had so quickly given way to the sober reality of recession gloom and the incredible horror of seeing the foreshadow of that Second World War.

The only bit of celebration was an odd victory ball or dance, and the flags put out at windows or gate-posts when a boy or girl came home for good.

Like other big exhausted cities and ageing villages, Glasgow took a long time to pick up its steady, prosperous heartbeat again.

We werenae wed until 1952, seven years after the war and we'd still ration books. I mind specially because you'd to hand them in, in your pre-wedding names, at your honeymoon boarding-house and so everyone knew you were honeymooning . . . or maybe wondered *if*.

And then, you see, our tenement house was furnished with the standard utility furniture and sheets an' that. I've got some still. Most cups and saucers were plain white wally and if you got a wee bit decoration on your weddin' china, you treated it like best Crown Derby.

Anyone who lived through the darg and destruction of war, either at the beginning or the middle of the twentieth century, could surely only yearn to see it end without another one.

Medals dinnae compe'sate you, for seventy year of your lungs still pechin' from the gas, or shufflin' along wi' gammy legs.

Nor for seeing the poppies blow among endless rows of crosses where the friends of your green years lie buried.

24

ALL FLAGS AND BUNTING

Ask your average Glaswegian who calls himself the man in the street what he thinks of the royal family and he'll be quick enough to tell you 'no' much', and that an hour spent in a drizzle or jooking behind somebody else's head to catch a glimpse of a royal is an hour wasted. But press him and he can tell you the exact hour and very spot he was standing on, the day he saw a king or queen, any or of their kin.

When very old man tells you the tales of his grandfather, who was even older when he died, and whom he knew as a young lad, you get a distinct sniff of the lang-syne middle ages! There must be a few still alive who just remember Queen Victoria, but Alick Murdoch's grandfather gave him a second-hand glimpse of an even earlier day than hers.

> My grandfather was coachman to the Marquis of Bute, sometime about the 1830s. That was at Rothesay and most of the time he'd to drive the family about the island yonder. But sometimes they took the carriage by ferry across the Firth of Clyde and up the old road to Glasgow. Then, come the 'season', they used to go up to London, changin' the horses right-enough, at post-houses or coachin' inns on the way. Many's the tale I had off my grandfather when I was young and I mind him comin' away wi' a story about one time when they were in London for the season.
>
> He took Miss Stuart (that was the marquis's sister) to this society revel at a house some way out at Richmond. He halted the carriage in the driveway and handed Miss Stuart down the step and saw she was escorted into the big house.

'Then,' says Grandpa, 'I was standin' wi' the carriage chattin' among all the other coachmen in their liveries, when a braw carriage arrives and a couple gets out.' The gent peers at the Bute coat-of-arms on the side of Grandfather's machine and looks up. 'Afternoon Sir,' says Grandpa. 'Afternoon,' says the gent. 'You in charge of this carriage?'

and the 95-year-old grandson draws himself up in his chair and speaks, all haughty and clipped, as he sees and hears the gentryman addressing the Clyde-born coachman 150 years earlier.

'Aye Sir.'

'Lord Bute's I see. I take it then that Bute has already gone inside?'

'No Sir, His Lordship's sister Miss Stuart . . .'

Then, my grandfather said, they spoke a wee while about the road down from Glasgow, and the gent asks if the Butes are goin' on well . . . so on an' so forth. Then he turns to his wife.

'Well, there you are my dear, you can chat with Miss Stuart inside . . . thank you, coachman.'

And again Mr Alick Murdoch draws himself up, every inch the lordship.

The couple goes up the steps and Grandpa turns back to his friends.

'What did he say to you?' they want to know.

'Just asked gin it was the Bute coach and after the health of the family,' says Grandfather.

'That was the king you were talking to, you know!'

I knew my grandfather well. I'm ninety-five and he lived to ninety-six and he told me to mind and tell my grandweans that he'd spoken wi' King William IV.

Alexander Brown wasn't a gentleman's coachman all his life. Not at all. From the island of Bute he took a shrewd look at what was happening on the Clyde and saw the trickle of wealthy Glasgow merchants, who had begun to tak' tent of the bonnie clachans on the Firth, grow to a steady stream, followed by boatloads of lesser citizens taking up the new fashion of installing their families in rented accommodation for holidays. Alexander counted his bawbees, took a lease on Kirn pier and bought a pair of cottages at the pierhead. Mansions and villas had to be heated and they had to be let from time to time. He set up as coal merchant and factor and soon he himself was quite the up-and-coming businessman in Kirn. But that was not all . . .

Grandpa wasnae done yet. He began to charter yachts for the merchant 'lairds' and their visitors and he started a wee yacht club. Nothin' very grand. But then he thought that considerin' he'd once met the queen's uncle at Richmond he and his friends had some sort of nodding acquaintance wi' her son the Prince of Wales, and so they might could ask him to come and sail on the Clyde . . . give it his royal patronage . . . They werenae blate, mind, were they? Anyway, maybe the prince was a wee bit amused at the quaint invitation. Well, he came and he enjoyed the Firth . . . it's a bonnie place, mind you. So you see yachting on the Clyde became quite the thing for the prince's friends and hangers-on. And what had been my grandpa's wee club, began to run the famous Royal Yacht Races, and we got to see the Prince of Wales quite often on the Clyde.

Another haunt of royals has always been the north-east of Scotland and the same prince, from time to time, found himself there to refresh himself for the rigours of his London social life or his yachting on the Clyde.

Glasgow has been home to Mr Harry Anderson for many years but his roots are in Golspie and so too are some of his inherited memories.

Queen Victoria was often a guest at Dunrobin Castle with the Duchess of Sutherland and the Prince of Wales used to come sometimes too. My grandfather was a tailor in Golspie so he used to get orders to make clothes for the prince, country-gentleman sort of clothes for wearing about the estates there.

All that was still in the mid-years of the century before Edward came into his inheritance and long before his mother's Diamond Jubilee in 1897 . . . an occasion never forgotten by the lady who was five-year-old Maggie Anderson in Uddingston that year.

I mind of Queen Victoria. I saw her once. She came in her carriage when I was just young. It was at her Jubilee time and we were all in the park wi' our wee flags to wave. She was a dumpy wee body, very proud I thought she was, for she just bowed a wee bit from her head. A' in black she was, and wearing a bonnet tied wi' ribbons in a black bow under her chin. She was very very old . . .

but nearly twenty years younger than the little flag-waving Maggie of those days is as she recollects that day.

Others had more official roles on that Jubilee visit. An old lady produces a spiked helmet. Her father, she explains, was in the queen's cavalry escort through the city and she has kept his helmet for eighty-seven of her ninety-six years.

He'd a grey horse, I think, and I was taken into the town to watch them passing. I was so busy looking at my father that I near didnae see Her. I mind thinkin' she wasnae much to look at anyway, compared wi' him and his glitterin' helmet. She'd no crown or jewels or anythin'. She was just wee and pudgy and dressed in black. At home they were cross wi' me and said she was a great lady, a queen and an empress and suchlike. Maybe she was, but I still thought she was wee and pudgy.

Many remember that 1897 visit to Glasgow, but fewer recall in detail the old queen's death four years later, perhaps because it happened far away in Osborne House and word of it came to children only in wae echoes of the grown-ups' hushed voices. That's how Miss Marie Condie remembers it.

My memory of Queen Victoria's death is just shadowy. I was a wee lassie at Merry Street school and the teachers were talkin' yon way in low voices about someone that had died. Then it was all explained to me at home that it was the queen that had died, that's picture was up on the parlour wall . . . When I think back I'm sure they were all wonderin' how it was to be, with Victoria no' there, and just the Prince of Wales.

On the other hand there was much more to remember about Edward's coronation, and there are souvenirs a-plenty to show for it.

I have this perfect clear memory of a picnic we had at the time of Edward and Alexandra's coronation. I've got this picture in my mind of a big, big brown Clydesdale horse wi' its bushy feet, standin'

> hitched up to just an ordinary cart that had seats across it wi' a safety-board thing round the sides . . . and it full of us weans. I had a tin mug on a blue ribbon round my neck, and what I mind, clear as clear, was us all squealin' and laughin' when we moved away. That's all I can think on about that coronation, except we got medals as well.

And Kate Thomas's memory of the same event.

> I mind Edward the Seventh's crownin' was delayed because he'd the appendicitis, but when it did come off, it was all flags and bunting and we got mugs wi' the king and queen on them. There's mine's there in the display cabinet.

There were coronation visits too, up and down the country, for Edward and Alexandra to show themselves off to their people as king and queen at long last, after what had seemed an interminable apprenticeship. Some visits they made together, some separately. Mrs Jean Tait remembers one of them.

> My father was a kind of big shot in the gardening world and he was asked to organise the floral decorations for Queen Alexandra's visit and I distinctly remember that he did them mainly in pink.
>
> There was a red carpet too and my mother got it afterwards and made it into a real nice cover for the dining room table. But even better I remembered what happened to me. Because of my father, we got a seat at an open window above the street and I was all dressed up in my good dress and best beads to watch the queen and the procession going by. Well, a band was playing, and there was me, beating time to the music and twirling my string of beads round my finger. Then just as the queen's carriage passed under the window, the string broke. The beads bounced off the window sill and mercy me! . . . there was the queen's hat right below. I heard my mother calling it a 'toque' but I just remember that it seemed to be made up entirely of violets. No brim, of course. The royal ladies never wore brims. Anyway if the beads were in among the violets that would be a wee surprise for Queen Alexandra when she took her hat off.

To mark Edward's death, eight short years later, most Glasgow children, like their parents, attended memorial services. Tokens of mourning too were worn by the general public for months afterwards, even by children like young Dorothy Laurie.

> Everyone wore some wee bit of mourning, black armbands or small black diamonds sewn on to your coat sleeves. I was ten years old and I mind of having a white coat at the time and a nice white boater-hat to go with it, but I had to wear a black band round the hat when the king died and I wasn't very pleased.

The black bands and mourning diamonds were scarcely unpicked from the 1910 braws, when it was time for the coronation of the quiet George V and his queen. The wally mugs, the medallions, the streamers and the cart-horse ribbons were ready in Glasgow and its surrounding cluster of boroughs. Picnics and parties were organised, concerts and pageants rehearsed in a hundred church halls and classrooms.

> When the new king came to Glasgow I went to Scotland Street to see him going past. I was that small I could hardly see him. I just got a glimpse of a man with a brown beard, but I waved my wee Union Jack like mad.

Young May Reid too had good reason to remember that coronation for the regal part she played in the celebrations.

> We'd a concert in the school with a tableau at the end . . . and here I was Britannia! Now my mother wasn't really a very dressy person but oh my, she was proud of me over the pageant! 'You're going to be just right, May. None of your old sheets and silver paper.'
>
> She took me to Josephine Smith's the theatrical costumière. She'd likely enough laid in a few dozen Britannia sets that spring. Anyway I got the whole jing-bang that was on the new penny, helmet, trident, shield and all. I always had lovely long hair away-way past my waist and it was usually in pig-tails. But for the concert it was all combed out and rippling over my shoulders. I had to sit high and prominent, and all the children representing other countries had to come in from the sides and bow to *me*. I was up on a step-ladder draped with cloth . . . purple I think . . . and there was me up top.
>
> I was the centre-piece and I thought I was great. Mind nowadays I'd like to believe all yon bowing was just because it was our

coronation, and if it had been, say, the king of Spain, *we* would've been bowing to him. But I don't think so . . . I mean to say, we did have all the pink bits on the map in 1911, sure we had?

George V was a sober monarch, after his galravaitching father, and not much noted for his bonhomie, but one Glasgow man did remember at least a chuckle from the king and passed on word of the incident to his family.

It was my grandfather came home this day and told us about being with George V when he was getting the freedom of the city . . . a right big Glasgow celebration that was. Anyway it was my grandpa's job that day to be in attendance with the king in an ante-room. He wrote all this down mind as well, so I can tell you pretty exact what happened. Here's what Grandpa says.

'I was alone with the king for quite a while and we had a wee bit conversation. He was quite easy and chatty and I told him that when my uncle was a worker at Loch Katrine water-works he'd got the job of giving Queen Victoria a cup of tea the day of the opening in 1852. My uncle always made his brew-up special by putting in a wee tate baking soda (maybe he didnae trust the new water). Anyway, George V had to smile at the idea of his granny drinking the bicarby tea on a public occasion. After that George V was quite jovial that day.'

But life wasn't all flags and bunting for King George and Queen Mary, not in their private lives at least. Their ailing youngest son, John, is not much remembered now but there are those who do passingly recall that he lived through childhood into adolescence.

I always mind of comin' out the pictures one night, maybe a year or so after the First World War, and hearin' the newsboys shout . . .
'*Times, News, Cit — iz — en* Prince John dies!
Times, News, Cit — iz — en Death of king's son!'

The eldest son, on the other hand, was very much alive, and like enough to his grandfather to give twinges of unease to his strict father. The prince was charming and immensely popular, and people waited with affectionate but disapproving interest, to see which of the string of ladies in his life would become the Princess of Wales. Miss Marie Condie felt that she was getting a more personal keek at some of the action than most people.

> I went to America in the 1920s to do a bit nursing there and see what-like it was. I sailed from the Broomielaw with my wee letter of introduction to the chief steward that I'd got from a friend of a friend. Anyway I got to know him quite well and we got to see round the boat. At the time the Prince of Wales was friendly with the actress, June, and they had dances and parties on board. So here, this steward said he would give me a present of something Edward had used. He offered me a choice of coffee cups, sweet dishes or a cushion. I don't know if he'd any right to do the likes of that, but I wasnae goin' to turn down the chance. It was maybe funny, but I chose the cushion for I knew it wouldnae break . . . the cushion cover's done long ago, but what you might call the Prince of Wales's feathers are there in the very pillow I still use.

Others saw him in his young-god heyday.

> I seen the Prince of Wales once in the 1930s when he was comin' along Pollokshaws Road standin' in an open car. I couldnae mind ever seeing even a picture of a king before wi' no beard or whiskers (and he was near-enough king). He was handsome, this blond chap, a lot younger-lookin' than he really was, and awful shy and embarrassed lookin'. Mind I don't think he was all that shy!

But there were a few years left to George and Mary before the dashing, clean-shaven prince became king. There were two royal weddings and the new interest of seeing the two little princesses, Elizabeth and Margaret Rose beginning to emerge on occasion into the public eye. But the climax to the reign was the celebration of the Silver Jubilee. There may have been different souvenirs but Glasgow did its weans proud by giving each a silver-coloured tin of toffees with pictures of the king and queen on the lid, and putting on firework displays.

Another year brought the end of the reign.

> I've never forgot hearin' on the wireless about 'the king's life drawin' slowly to its close'. I was just nine then, and I was a Brownie. We'd to

wear a thin black braid like an armband on our wee cotton uniforms. I thought it was all awful sad wi' the black edges to *The Bulletin* and the slow dreich music on the wireless. I mind of seeing the funeral at the pictures and yon horses bobbin' along wi' the black plumes, and I mind seein' the new king, and his three brothers followin' the coffin.

The general public knew nothing then about the storm to come and, respectful sadness for George V over, it looked forward to having a modern king genuinely interested in the lives of his people. When Edward VIII came to Glasgow on a private visit about that time and drove through the city to stay with his friends the Weir family at Eastwood Park, people looked at his pale, set face and hoped they saw high purpose in it.

I saw him arriving at the park. I mind him sitting in the back of a great big car. He was good-lookin' but his face was awful white and kind of glum. All the same he gave a wee stiff smile and waved to the handful of folk standin' there at the lodge gate.

There were other reasons of course for the serious face and, as 1936 wore on, people began to talk, and the young couldn't help but overhear.

I was nine years old then and and I loved Edward. I collected pictures of him and read all about him. But I was right miserable when I heard the grown-ups talk and knew he was in some kind of disgrace (though I had an uncle that thought it was everyone else that was the disgrace). I've still got the newspaper picture of him sittin' at the microphone talkin' on the wireless, all sad and tired, about 'the woman I love'. Fifty years old, it is, that picture, and a bit yellow, but I'll no part with it . . . I've got a kind of non-memento too . . . an Edward VIII coronation mug.

But loyalty is fickle and sadness put away with photographs. The Duke of York was the new hero, the new king with his comprehensible lifestyle and his family.

I saw the king and queen when they came to Glasgow not long after their coronation. I stood in Argyle Street and they came by in a high car, or maybe it was a carriage. They were lovely!

Of all the Glasgow folk who have cast their minds back for this book to the coronation of 1937, when they were school bairns, at least half still keep dominoes, buttons or other trinkets in the square blue assorted toffees tin handed out to them by some genial councillor, as they filed past him in their school hall.

It was a century since a child had been heir to the British throne and the sensibly rare public appearances of Princess Elizabeth and her sister were the better remembered for their rarity. Glasgow caught one such glimpse when they came to the Empire Exhibition in 1938.

> I mind I saw the princesses there. I can just see them yet, look-ing as if they didnae know what it was all about, and wished they were back home wi' Crawfie. Maybe they were enjoyin' it all fine right enough but they didnae look like it, sittin' up prim in their wee pink coats and hats and other weans screamin' wi' fun on the helter-skelter. I mind seein' Princess Marina and the Duke of Kent at the Exhibition too; they said he'd make-up on his face but I thought he was very handsome.

Royal memories of the war years are sparse. Recollections are of other matters than public appearances and junketings. There must be veteran servicemen and women who cherish a word spoken by a king who was tiring too young or a sighting of his sparkling queen in her brave wartime braws, but none have reminisced for this book. But Mrs Janet Purvis has one memory of the days just after the war.

> I was awarded the City of Glasgow medal for the nursing I did in the war and the presentation was at the City Chambers. I remem-ber we drank tea from real Crown Derby china. Then the queen gave me my medal. The invitation said to dress simply because, you see, clothes were still on coupons. But our gloves had to be *pristine* white.

And the rememberer in her high-backed chair enunciated the word like a royal curtsey, and repeated it.

Pristine! I had a very nice ensemble, black, with grey fox fur round the hem and cuffs, and I had a black polished-straw hat from Daly's, with two marguerites at one side and a wee drift of veiling.

Simple? Perhaps not. But used no doubt for a long time and kept in memory for ever.

Since those days royal personages have become more visible and more approachable. Encounters are more frequent and delight most ordinary mortals, apart from those whose teeth are set on edge by their mere existence. But recollections about the present royals are no great test of memory and we can leave such reminiscences to mature until they are the stuff of nostalgia and ready to be told to some collector of tales 100 years from now.